"If you ever struggle with loneliness, you'll love this book! *The New Loneliness* offers biblical solutions to the pain loneliness brings. Filled with comfort, encouragement, and Cindi's relatable trademark wisdom, you'll walk away feeling seen, understood, and most of all, equipped to see how God can fill your deepest longings."

—**Donna Jones**, author of *Healthy Conflict, Peaceful Life*; host of *That's Just What I Needed* podcast

"Cindi McMenamin has undertaken the timely topic of loneliness in a world where people are counted as 'friends' on social media. She shares examples that illustrate how a community of believers can and have provided true friendships by relating with people face to face. This is a well-timed book to have in your library; I have it in mine."

—**Gail Cawley Showalter**, author of *Living, Learning, Loving*

"Are you weary of the pretense of community in today's culture? Does the threat of being cancelled keep you from being real in your online relationships? You are not alone. At a time when society is most connected, loneliness is at its peak. It's time to change that. And the change begins with you. In *The New Loneliness*, Cindi McMenamin insightfully unpacks the reasons you feel lonely, and more importantly, shows you practical ways to intentionally create connections that will last a lifetime."

—**Rhonda Stoppe**, founder of No Regrets Woman; author of *Moms Raising Sons to Be Men*, *If My Husband Would Change I'd Be Happy*, and *Real-Life Romance*

"Cindi masterfully nails the serious problem of the new loneliness, a relentless companion for young and old alike. Loneliness flows like a poisoned river—contaminated with the isolation of shame, the crush of busyness, the pain of suffering, the endless scrolling of screen time, and more. I drank from that poisoned river for many years before God stemmed its flow through His transforming Word of truth. In *The New Loneliness*, you'll discover how God's Word can help you connect in closer companionship with Him, create a more biblical version of yourself, and build valuable relationships that comfort and encourage you. Like Cindi, you'll find your loneliness is not pointless when
C

uthor of *Truth Talk for Hurting Hearts*;
ices Today and Truth Talk with Dawn

"Cindi McMenamin's books are always powerful explorations of how God wants to be involved in our lives. In this exemplary book, Cindi not only points to the problems and causes of loneliness but gives us godly, empowering wisdom for connecting with God, our own hearts, and other people. I love her personal stories, which help make truth applicable. I especially appreciate each chapter's 'Being Intentional' section, which is like a combined Bible study and journal. Read this book and face your loneliness confidently, or prepare your heart for times of being lonely."

—**Kathy Collard Miller**, international speaker;
author of 60 books, including *Anger Management—Jesus Style*

"Cindi zeroes in on the almost-worldwide affliction of a new kind of loneliness that has produced unwanted depths of emotional isolation. Drawing insights from real-life situations and illuminating biblical perspectives, she offers lifelines through every chapter and reminds us that God assures we can thrive through immense challenges. Cindi's 'key seeds'—verses like Philippians 4:6-7, and her recurring theme that God is with us, is for us, and creates purpose in us—are sown throughout the book."

—**Jeannie Linderman**, Bible teacher; cocreator of
Fresh Start—Evangelical Bible Foundations Study

"There is a high cost when you exchange interpersonal relationships for internet relationships. We may be connected to people around the world through our phones, but day-to-day life has become increasingly lonely. How can we grow closer to God through seasons of loneliness and live in fellowship with others again? Cindi McMenamin offers a book of hope and help for anyone who feels lonely today."

—**Arlene Pellicane**, speaker; host of the *Happy Home* podcast; author of
Calm, Cool, and Connected: 5 Digital Habits for a More Balanced Life

"*The New Loneliness* is an amazing book that will equip and encourage you with practical ways to apply faith-filled steps to move forward from loneliness to trusting others in new ways. It will empower you to live in a new mindset as you begin trusting in your growing relationships with God and others. This book will change your day, life, and godly relationships with friends and family."

—**Jayme Hull**, mentor expert and spiritual direction coach

THE
NEW
LONELINESS

CINDI McMENAMIN

HARVEST HOUSE PUBLISHERS
EUGENE. OREGON

Cover design by Bryce Williamson

Cover images © Victoria Gnatiuk / Getty Images

Interior design by KUHN Design Group

For bulk, special sales, or ministry purchases, please call 1-800-547-8979.
Email: CustomerService@hhpbooks.com

M This logo is a federally registered trademark of the Hawkins Children's LLC. Harvest House Publishers, Inc., is the exclusive licensee of this trademark.

This book includes accounts in which the author has changed people's names and some details of their situations in order to protect their privacy.

The information presented in this book is meant to be used for general resource purposes only. It is not intended to serve as a mental health or medical guide, nor should it substitute medical advice from a health care professional. If you have or think you may have a medical problem, speak to your doctor or health care practitioner immediately about your risk and possible treatments. Do not engage in any therapy or treatment without consulting a mental health or medical professional.

The New Loneliness
Copyright © 2024 by Cindi McMenamin
Published by Harvest House Publishers
Eugene, Oregon 97408
www.harvesthousepublishers.com

ISBN 978-0-7369-8964-0 (pbk)
ISBN 978-0-7369-8965-7 (eBook)

Library of Congress Control Number: 2024935677

Printed in the United States of America

24 25 26 27 28 29 30 31 32 / BP / 10 9 8 7 6 5 4 3 2 1

For my mom, who will never know loneliness again.

CONTENTS

ADDITIONAL RESOURCES

HOW DID
WE GET HERE?

Defining the New Loneliness

Are you feeling lonelier these days than you used to? Experiencing that unexplainable ache you can't seem to get rid of? Perhaps you're spending more time with your phone than with people and you don't want to think about how that might've happened. Maybe you used to feel closer to God and some of your friends and family than you do today, and you don't know how to reverse that. You could be feeling on the outside of popular opinion or wondering if you have a place or voice in today's culture or even in your own family. Or, perhaps you wish you had a church or were more connected at the one you attend.

You're not the only one feeling lonelier than ever. Loneliness has always been a struggle for many of us and continues to be. But in recent decades, the causes of loneliness have multiplied. A lot has shifted in the world around us, and there is a new loneliness afloat, making the problem more pervasive than ever. In addition to living in an increasingly high-tech and screen-focused society, we've been impacted by the forced isolation from the COVID-19 pandemic lockdowns that persisted for nearly two years all around us. The lockdowns pushed our culture's reliance on tech and screens even more. Video conferencing alone has forever changed the way many of us operate—at work, in schools, at church, and in our homes.

While the pandemic is now behind us, our increased reliance upon AI, high tech, and screens isn't. And the habits formulated over an extended time of isolation and caution have led us into a new and different normal. Without necessarily intending to do so, we've all become more acclimated to new habits and new ways of going about life. We've adapted, but the results of our new normal have had a profound impact on us and aren't all positive.

Both technology and the consequences of the pandemic have taken us to a place where the traditional kinds of loneliness we've struggled with—loneliness caused by anxiety, shame, suffering, feelings of inadequacy, betrayal, and more—have become increasingly pronounced. The kinds of loneliness that have always plagued humanity since the Garden of Eden are still with us. But now we have new obstacles and complications that have contributed to isolating us from others. And these have made loneliness more a part of our lives.

In mid-2023, the US Surgeon General issued a health alert that confirmed there is an *"epidemic* of loneliness"—a health risk of isolation (which includes spending more time with screens than people), and a failure to connect deeply with others through friendships and risk of intimacy—that is now increasing your chance of dementia by 50 percent and your chance of premature death by more than 60 percent. It is actually *unhealthy* to be lonely today—mentally, emotionally, spiritually, and now physically, regardless of your age. According to the Surgeon General, the long-term health risks of loneliness are equivalent to the danger of smoking up to 15 cigarettes a day![1]

As I mentioned earlier, people have always suffered from loneliness. We have *all* felt it now and then. But now it's more persistent. And these more intense feelings of loneliness didn't happen overnight.

There has been a *progression of loneliness* for people in general over the past two decades, and more intensely the past five years.

The convenience of online everything has contributed to this, making it possible for you and me to not leave our home for days. Virtual meetings—which have become increasingly more convenient, time-efficient, and money-saving—have made us more comfortable sitting in front of a screen than interacting with people face to face. Hitting a "Leave Meeting" button (rather than exiting a room politely by saying your goodbyes) has made what used to be general courtesy and relationship-building behavior now seem like an unnecessary waste of time. Everyone has their work to do, right? Few people have time to talk instead of text. Stick to the work at hand. Refrain from speaking, opening up, or even starting a conversation. Avoid eye contact—everyone does. And most of us don't even realize it. The result? Fewer conversations. Even less transparency. Next to zero relationships. Loneliness.

In this book, we're going to look at the kinds of loneliness that we all experience. And we're going to do so with an awareness that the "traditional" forms of loneliness now have to contend with the new normal.

THE TYPES OF LONELINESS

With that in mind, see if you can find yourself—or your type of loneliness—in one or more of these real women's stories. As you read along, consider how today's new normal can aggravate the loneliness these women are feeling.

The Loneliness of Feeling Overwhelmed

As a new mom, Janie feels overwhelmed and inadequate as she wades through the different suggestions, personal opinions, and online advice on what would be best for her child.

"Personally, I feel alone when I make wrong choices," she said. "I feel alone when I need to make an important decision for my child and there is no right or wrong answer. There isn't anyone to walk me through the correct answer because there are negatives on both sides. This also makes me feel inadequate because I don't feel confident in either choice."

And Janie feels particularly lonely when her husband is not sharing parenting responsibilities with her and "when my kids are needing all of me when all I need is a break."

Oh, the loneliness of feeling overwhelmed and constantly wondering if you're getting it right.

The Loneliness of Comparison

Alexa is a young wife and mom who is bright, capable, and a ray of sunshine to all who interact with her. But she doesn't see herself that way. She admits that watching others' highlight reels on social media can make her think she's constantly missing out or lagging behind.

"Comparing myself to others around the same age or stage of my life and seeing all of their accomplishments makes me feel like I haven't done enough," Alexa said. "I also feel guilty for my lack of community and intentional time spent with others." Having a different set of values and convictions than those around her, which can be accentuated these days by comments and responses on social media, also makes her feel especially lonely.

The Loneliness of Internal Struggles

Kadee has a personal relationship with Jesus, a godly husband who is a leader in their church, and five healthy children. She recently received her master's degree in social work. But Kadee struggles with that negative internal voice—a combination of hurtful things said to her in the past, her own inner critic, and taunting from the enemy of her soul—that convinces her, at times, that everyone else would be better off without her. She knows her worth in God's eyes, and she is intentional about involving herself in Bible study groups and surrounding herself with godly mentors who help her continue to grow spiritually. Yet she still struggles with what is now diagnosed as mental illness—a tendency toward anxiety, depression, and self-harm.

"Personally, I feel like there isn't anyone who could understand what I'm going through," Kadee told me recently.

The Loneliness of Feeling Judged

Sherrill is still feeling the sting of loneliness after losing her church family a few years ago due to growing differences of opinion within her congregation that were based more on personal beliefs than Scripture. Her eyes were opened to how quickly people can divide over political and emotional issues and she's been struggling to find a safe, nonjudgmental place to worship ever since.

"I feel like the destruction of the relationships within my former church family has touched every area of my life and has caused a deep distress and loneliness," she said. "I know God is with me, but I know He created us for community as well. The loss of Christian community and not knowing exactly where I fit in anymore has been a lonely road these past few years."

The Loneliness of Failed Friendships

Jenna believed nothing could separate her from her BFF. She and SueAnn were soulmates, partners in ministry, true sisters at heart. Until the day SueAnn started slowly backing away. A tension crept in between them and Jenna couldn't understand why. SueAnn didn't want to talk about it. She kept saying she was busy or unavailable for time with Jenna. Finally, SueAnn told Jenna she was tired of feeling she couldn't compete or be half as good as Jenna in most areas of her life. Jenna felt devastated that her friend would turn on her for something she didn't feel she could do anything about. She spent the summer seeking solace in her relationship with God, and wondering whether she could ever trust another friend to get close to her.

What loneliness we can feel when we lose a friend or find we suddenly have much less openness than we used to with someone we loved and trusted.

WHAT IS *YOUR* LONELINESS FACTOR?

Loneliness can rear its ugly head through any number of circumstances, or through unresolved wounds that lie festering in our hearts. It can blow in during a season of being overwhelmed and feeling we have no one to support us, or during a season of fruitlessness when we feel we're too old, or too worn out, or too inept to do what we used to. It can pull us down when we feel we're at the top of the world with everything we want in life, but we have no one to share it with. It can taunt us in the late hours of the evening when we feel, even if just for a while, that no one cares about us, or understands what we're dealing with. And it can slam us when we least expect it through a sudden betrayal, a sense of abandonment, or a deep wound that we fear might never heal.

Loneliness also has a way of creeping up on us unnoticed, as it did in my own life, through a series of subconscious and tech-enabled habits that lead us to one day look around and think, *Where have all my friends gone? Why am I suddenly more of a loner than I ever set out to be? How did this happen?*

Whether your loneliness is caused by your work or living circumstances, a misunderstanding or falling out with someone, unresolved conflict with family or friends, or feeling inadequate, unprepared, unsupported, or overwhelmed, we were never designed to live this way. In addition to a myriad of reasons we can feel increasingly lonely today, the ever-changing, continually isolating culture we live in isn't helping. It's making our loneliness worse.

OUR CHANGING
CULTURE — AND LANGUAGE

Regardless of what your circumstances look like, the loneliness is real. And ironically, this culture of convenience and all it seems to offer—including an increased sense of isolation—has robbed us of more than we realize. We even define ourselves and describe our feelings and activities today as if we are electronic devices instead of living, breathing, uniquely created individuals.

Think about it. When was the last time you said, or heard, something like "I'm on information overload, I just need to defrag," or "I'll need some time to recharge my battery" (and you weren't talking about your phone)? We are often encouraged to *plug into* a church and to *unplug* from our busyness. When we're high on adrenaline, we consider ourselves *wired*; when we're tired or burnt out, we say we're *fried* or we've *overloaded our circuits*.

In addition, our *interpersonal* relationships have gradually become outnumbered by our *internet* relationships. Face time used to mean what it sounds like, and it didn't involve a screen. *Social* used to mean *talking* or *being* with one another, not typing or scrolling on an electronic device. "Can we Zoom about this later?" you might find yourself saying. "I don't have the emotional or mental bandwidth for it right now."

Today we refer to ourselves—and our daily activities—in electronic terms to the point that we use Google as a verb and may feel more comfortable with our electronic devices than with one another. I can't help but wonder how much more alone that makes us feel—like objects rather than people, and digital codes rather than intricately designed creations. And the pandemic conditioned us in ways that make isolation seem more normal, more routine.

These factors give us even more to overcome when loneliness sets in.

TAKING TIME TO TALK — NOT TEXT

When was the last time you experienced a deep conversation with a friend on the phone or in person? When did you last express your heartfelt feelings about a topic, or inquire about what someone was thinking or reading and how it was impacting them? I've started doing that through handwritten letters I've been exchanging (yes, through snail mail) with my cousin. And it made me realize the depth of conversation that doesn't happen through text or even email. Sitting down to compile one's thoughts onto paper requires time to think and choose one's words carefully. No wonder letter-writing relationships can help people draw closer to one another. And no wonder they're nearly extinct today.

Can you remember when you last shared your heart over coffee or a meal and teared up — or witnessed a pool of tears well up in your friend's eyes — as you each peeled back another layer of your personalities or wounds and were willing to be vulnerable with one another? When was the last time you discussed with a friend the meaning of a certain Scripture passage or what God has been doing in their life or yours? How long has it been since you drove home after a conversation with a friend, reflecting upon the discussion and anticipating when you could meet again face to face to talk more?

Opportunities for truly openhearted interaction don't happen much anymore and rarely at random. There's an intentionality that is being lost in the midst of our busyness, the convenience of text messaging, the "normalcy" of isolation, or the desire to stay somewhat less transparent for fear of the emotional energy — and possible rejection — of going deeper with who we are and how we feel. Sometimes we might back off of expressing ourselves or saying what we really feel about a subject for fear that what we say won't be deemed politically correct or might unintentionally offend someone. Social media has taught us to guard our opinions or we might be unfriended or cancelled.

If you and I continue to fear backlash, prioritize productivity over people, prefer screens to faces, become online spectators rather than real-life participants, or fear a deeper emotional level with someone else, we will pay an even costlier price in the form of increased loneliness. And if we prefer to soak up information and answers from Google rather than God's Word, resulting in no longer challenging our minds to really think through an issue (and pray through it as well), we will live like our devices—cold, quick, devoid of feeling and emotion, and constantly in need of recharging.

HOW IT'S IMPACTING US

Multiple studies have confirmed that, regardless of our age, prolonged screen time, extensive social media use, and lack of interpersonal contact with other humans are greatly impacting our anxiety and depression levels as well as our ability to know how to develop and navigate deeper connections with other humans.* Add to this the fact that we live in a world in which people are becoming increasingly self-centered and narcissistic, partly due to social media (which gives everyone a chance to be "on stage"), and partly because of how society has shaped us to be self-focused rather than people-focused. Although today's preteens and teenagers are at the greatest mental health risk from prolonged screen time, every one of us who owns a smartphone or scrolling device is subject to being lured into a preference of virtual over reality, online observation rather than personal participation, texting rather than talking, and making a transaction or decision online rather than with the help of another human. We can claim the advantages of high tech, but the bottom line is we've found one more way to move further from personal interaction. We've added another layer to our loneliness problem. We've found one more way to increase our anxiety and depression levels.

---

* I will present the findings of some of these studies in chapter 8, "The Loneliness of Screens."

The result of all this tech gone wild and unhealthy reliance on the digital rather than flesh and blood? Loneliness—to a degree we've never seen before. While tech in and of itself isn't bad, an unhealthy reliance on it that replaces human touch cannot help but impact us.

But friend, you don't have to be a victim of what is happening in our culture. You don't have to be another loneliness, anxiety, or depression statistic that is worsening daily. You can rise above this by knowing Who is *with* you, Who is *for* you, and why you are here. You can make a much-needed trajectory change when you embrace the resources (and people) available to help you soar rather than suffer silently.

WHERE IS THE DIFFERENCE?

When you and I realize that we exist not to work or perform certain tasks (like an electronic device) but to reflect the glory of our loving Maker—and to enjoy His presence and the communion of other like-minded believers—it will transform our lives. We will not only understand who we are and why we're here, but we will revel in our purpose, which involves so much more than producing, performing, pleasing others, or attaining perfection. We will be able to experience fulfillment and joy—and where that exists, there is no room for loneliness.

But wait! Loneliness should only happen to people who don't know God, you may be thinking. *Why is it happening to me? Isn't God supposed to prevent these feelings of loneliness because He said He would never leave me nor forsake me? Isn't He supposed to provide for all my needs, including companionship and emotional support? Why can't I just pray and make these feelings of loneliness go away?*

Loneliness will always exist as long as you and I are looking for something outside the realm of what God already offers us. Do you realize that—even though we live in a world that constantly disappoints, where sin has damaged our lives and the lives of those we love—Jesus has *already* provided us with everything we need this side of heaven to live a fulfilling, joyful life in Him? He has *already* provided us with companionship, encouragement, support, personal affirmation, and a sense of self-worth and purpose.

How can you embrace all that has been provided for you through a relationship with the living God and those He brings your way? How can you experience the joy and *immeasurably more* Jesus came to give you and not succumb to this culture of isolationism? How can you live like a loved daughter of God, exuding the confidence that comes from being closely connected to your Maker and a spiritual family who supports you? That's what we're going to look at together in this book.

But before we proceed any further, it's time to ask yourself some questions.

HOW LONELY ARE *YOU*?

Turn to page 235 and take a few minutes to complete a brief self-assessment test to help you determine the likely degree to which this epidemic of loneliness has affected you. You may discover some things about yourself that you hadn't yet realized. After answering each question, come back here. (Please don't skip this part. It's super important, and you'll gain more insight into your loneliness factor and what might be contributing to it.) Go to page 235 now, and I'll meet you back here in a bit.

OUR NEXT STEP

Perhaps as you answered the questions in the self-assessment test, you were able to gauge your social, emotional, and spiritual health, or maybe get a better idea of your friendship factor—or how it can improve. While those results are certainly not all-conclusive, perhaps you realized, based on some of your answers, that a rerouting of your heart needs to happen, or a change of habits might be helpful. Maybe some initiation on your part or some risk-taking is in order as you focus more on God and other people in your life. Perhaps there is some pain that needs to be addressed and surrendered to God so you can learn to trust again. And it's possible there are some relationships you can foster, return to, or begin to develop altogether. Sometimes it's a matter of merely putting away our phones and focusing on our relationships with God and the people who are right in front of us.

To solve our loneliness problem, you and I need more than another ten friends on our social media platforms. We need more than another handful of hearts or thumbs-up emojis on our posts. We need more than well-intended advice to "go to church" or "read your Bible" (although those last two suggestions are a good *start* toward experiencing some life changes). You and I need a closer relationship with Jesus and a deeper connection with our sisters in Christ—one of the ways we can experience "Jesus with skin on."

Through the chapters in this book, I aim to share how you can connect more closely with God, with your own heart, and with women who can strengthen you personally and spiritually. I've divided this book into three sections:

1. Reconnecting with God

God is *with* you, He's *for* you, and He has a reason why you're here. When you reconnect—or start to *really* connect—with God, you'll find your value in Him, as well as the priority He set for your life—the one thing you're all about—to love Him with all your heart, mind, soul, and strength, and to love others as yourself (Matthew 22:37-39). When you better understand who you are and why you were created, you will be more equipped to resolve whatever is causing your feelings of loneliness.

2. Reconnecting with Your Heart

In chapters 4–7, we'll look at obstacles that can keep you from developing deeper friendships with others, whether it's your sense of inadequacy, your belief that you're too busy, your excessive time spent with your devices, or your hesitancy to become vulnerable and transparent with others because of trust issues or society's lie that you don't need anyone else but you. As you free your heart of what keeps it in bondage, you can more easily trust those whom God brings your way and start developing more meaningful relationships with them.

3. Reconnecting with Others

In these last three chapters, we'll look at how to personally connect (or in some cases reconnect) with others despite our overreliance on the convenience of screens and text messaging as well as our culture's increasing trends toward isolation. We'll look at how to push through the hesitation we may feel to forge friendships despite personality differences and misunderstandings that inevitably exist in the body of Christ. Finally, we'll look at how to be compassionate and forgiving followers of Jesus who can encourage, serve, and extend grace toward others in the kind of meaningful community God intended.

Each chapter will end with an application section called "Being Intentional." Here, I'll give you some time to go further in God's Word, along with a challenge to complete. Unless we are intentional about reconnecting with God and other people, it won't happen. God has already made the first move. I'll suggest practical ways you can respond to Him or make your next move toward reconnecting with others as another way of clearing loneliness out of your life.

It is my prayer this book will help move you forward out of a lonely life and into the abundant one Jesus promised when you're in relationship with Him and the community of believers He has placed around you. I want nothing more than for you to discover God's prescription for a far more joyful—and far less lonely—life.

Are you ready to open your heart so God can touch those broken, lonely places and expand your circle of friends? It's time to be brave, girlfriend. Let's see what the Maker of your soul has to say about who you are, why you're here, and the immeasurably more He has for you.

PART 1

RECONNECTING WITH GOD

Our path to a less-lonely life starts as we reconnect with God and consider Who He is and how that can make a difference in our lives. As we better understand His character and why He has us here, we will better know how to interpret feelings of loneliness that surface all too often.

Seeing the truth about God's heart for us is key to knowing how to live, love, and serve others in meaningful community and fulfilling relationships.

Let's look more closely at Who is with you, Who is for you, and the very beautiful reason He has for why you are here.

CHAPTER 1

THE LONELINESS
OF ANXIETY

Knowing Who Is *with* You

*The steadiness by which we walk secure in our journeys with Christ
has everything to do with our confidence in the character of God.*[1]

RUTH CHOU SIMONS

I found myself deeply disturbed this morning.

I read that "stress and anxiety levels have never been higher—in
our country, in our families, and *in our churches*."[2] Of course, look
around from day to day, and that alone shouldn't be a surprise.

But the fact that those of us who know God tend to be just as
stressed and anxious as those who don't saddened me. And it woke
me up to the anxious times we're living in.

The blog post stated that "there is always stress in our lives and
churches, but today's environment makes soaring anxiety difficult
to manage." It listed reasons we deal with more stress and anxiety
today, including

- increasing polarization;
- people taking hard stances politically on issues like race,
  police protection, and gender-driven issues;

- differing spiritual values;

- conflict and an inability to manage it;

- financial concerns; and

- a growing confusion about who we are and our purpose.[3]

While the article suggested internal investigation (which included asking yourself what you're anxious about), and then incorporating tips for a more balanced lifestyle (which included getting rest, exercising, and having a daily practice like meditation, keeping gratitude lists, and Bible study), what it *didn't* state is that *Who* we know and *how much we trust Him* can make all the difference in our anxiety and overall feelings of loneliness.

My mind began to race. *How can anyone who knows God begin to go down that road of being anxious? Is our theology now just theory, and not practical enough to produce any real changes in our lives and our ability to cope?*

And then, rather suddenly, I joined that segment of Christ-followers who become anxious.

My doctor had called, informing me that my blood test results 30 days after a minor surgery indicated I would need to go on a low-level medication. *For the rest of my life.*

As someone who has looked primarily to diet, exercise, and the power of prayer as the remedy to any ailment or attitude, I immediately became discouraged.

How could this have happened? My mind began its internal rant. *I was praying so hard that everything in my body would work normally after this surgery, and now I have to take a medication for the next 20 to 30 years?*

Then my inner critic took over.

This happened because you allowed yourself to get stressed and then sick. You weren't careful enough with your health, and now you're going to pay the cost.

Next, my sense of panic kicked in.

What do I do now? Do I start on the meds? Should I take natural supplements first and see if that will solve the problem? I don't have time to research this and make sure I'm doing it right—not while I'm trying to finish writing this book. I can't do this. I can't handle one more thing right now!

Amidst the stress, rising blood pressure, and a closing sensation in my throat, the truth of God's Word penetrated my situation like a light shining into a long, dark tunnel.

"Is anything too difficult for the LORD?" (Genesis 18:14).

"I have loved you with an everlasting love…I have drawn you out with kindness" (Jeremiah 31:3).

"I have searched you and known you…I am intimately acquainted with all your ways" (see Psalm 139:1-3).

"I will never leave you, nor will I ever forsake you" (see Hebrews 13:5).

As the truth of God's Word washed over my mind and drowned out my anxious thoughts, the truth of God's *character* softened my heart, slowed my pulse, and reminded me of what was true in that moment and always: My God is *with* me. This didn't take Him by surprise. And He will get me through this.

ANXIETY HAPPENS

How natural it is for you and me to go into a tailspin when circumstances feel overwhelming. When we can't see the future. How quickly we can panic and feel we must figure out our problems ourselves. How easy it is to rush ahead in our minds to the worst-case scenario, all the reasons to blame ourselves, and all the reasons we can't get through something. Yet how can you and I fear *anything* when we are under the watchful eye of the all-powerful, all-capable, and ever-loving God who has repeatedly proven that He will not let anything touch us that hasn't first passed through His loving hands?

Anxiety happens. And it can happen at any moment that you and I are not fully convinced that we are intensely loved, intimately cared for, and being capably moved forward into His perfect plan for us as we surrender our situation to Him.

Anxiety can take our hearts and minds hostage when we are not fully convinced that God is capable of taking care of whatever concerns us. While you and I can only see today (and we are experts about *fearing* tomorrow!), the God who holds all our days in His hands and has seen every one of them before us is waiting to lovingly and gently convince us that

- all His ways are perfect (Psalm 18:30)

- He knows how to give eternally good gifts to His children (Matthew 7:11)

- He will work *all things* together for good in our lives so that we will become more like His Son (Romans 8:28-29)

- He can give us His perfect peace that is beyond our understanding when we give our concerns to Him (Philippians 4:6-7)

- He will never leave us on our own (Psalm 139:7-12; Hebrews 13:5)

When I started focusing on my concerns and the circumstances I could not control, I slid into a state of stress and downward-spiraling worry, and realized I had one of two choices:

1. I could choose to feel neglected, discriminated against, and left to my own devices to figure this out (and the result would be continued stress, panic, fear, and full-blown anxiety).

2. Or I could call upon the One who loves me more than I can fathom and who is allowing me to go through this for a reason, and trust His goodness (resulting in the peace He promises to everyone who surrenders to Him in prayer).

I chose to give my situation to the Lord in prayer. I didn't give it to Him in a verbal vent. I *surrendered* it to Him, transferring it to His capable hands so I wouldn't be weighed down by it any longer, and thanking Him that it didn't take Him by surprise. And in return, God's promise to give His incomprehensible peace held true. His peace covered me like a warm blanket draped over my cold, worried heart. The worry and anxiety were gone.

Within a couple of minutes, I received a text message from Ashley, the research queen of natural supplements who has a voice that could calm a crying baby (which is what I was when I got her message). I hadn't heard from Ashley in six months, but that morning, she felt God's nudge on her heart to contact me and ask how I was doing in light of my recent surgery. We scheduled a time to meet for lunch a few days later. As I shared with Ashley my struggle, face to face, I let her know that her text message came at just the right time and that her listening ear, her comforting words, and her physical presence at lunch that day were reassuring gifts from God.

Our God is not only *with us* when we're stressed out, but there are times when He will also send His people our way to minister to our hearts when we most need it.

GOD ALREADY KNOWS

As you and I struggle with whatever is taking us down that lonely road of uncertainty or anxiety, God already knows what we need. But He often waits for us to surrender to Him our inability to work it out ourselves, and to come to Him with open arms ready to receive His help.

Through God's peaceful presence,* through His trustworthy Word, and through His body—our brothers and sisters in the Lord whose ears are tuned to hear His voice and detect His nudges—God will provide the guidance and wisdom you and I need to make every decision that is before us. You and I are not alone. Our God is *with us*.† And so are those He has surrounded us with, even when we're still feeling alone.

But we can tend to circumvent this process of trusting God's presence, looking to His Word for help, and reaching out to others in the body of Christ because we've been conditioned to consult Siri or Google for help, instead of the One who knows us intimately. Our reliance on tech can tend to interrupt our formerly instinctual response of going to God first. Could that be why we are more anxious today than we ever have been even though we have "expert advice" at our fingertips? By seeking to get the answers ourselves, on our devices, we are sometimes precluding prayer and the awareness that "God's got this" and entering the arena of feeling we're on our own. Perhaps we unknowingly assume it's more efficient to go online and search, rather than get on our knees and pray.

WHAT WE STRUGGLE WITH

I imagine you, too, struggle with the loneliness that comes from believing you are on your own at times, whether it's concerning your health, your finances, your love life (or lack of it), your marriage or relationships, your family issues, your children (and what they're going

---

* When we have surrendered our lives to Christ and accepted His sacrificial death for us on the cross, He sends His Holy Spirit to dwell within us, providing His comforting presence with us at all times (Ephesians 1:13 and 1 John 4:12-14). Sometimes we just aren't tuned in to the Spirit's voice or presence, so we forget He's there. But God promised His presence would never leave us. If you don't have the assurance that you have God's indwelling Holy Spirit, and therefore His guiding presence in your life, please turn to page 241 and read "How to Be Assured of God's Presence" before going any further.

† Matthew 1:23 tells us another name for Jesus is *Immanuel*, which literally means "God with us."

through or whether or not they're talking to you), or anything else. You, too, might feel you are left to your own devices (literally) and have no real live support system around you. Perhaps you feel as if you are sinking into a dark tunnel of despair where feelings of uncertainty or the "Why, Lord?" questions become too much.

But you and I don't have to remain stuck there, in that ache of loneliness, as we struggle. In fact, we don't even have to *go* there. God has already *been* there, and can help guide us back toward the light, where fear and anxiety no longer exist.

OUR PRESCRIPTION FOR ANXIETY

God knew we'd be an anxious people. He is aware of our weaknesses and our worries, and He told us in His Word, "Do not be anxious about anything, but in everything by prayer and pleading with thanksgiving let your requests be made known to God. And the peace of God, which surpasses all comprehension, will guard your hearts and minds in Christ Jesus" (Philippians 4:6-7). In a translation that incorporates the original Greek meaning into idiomatic English, which is the way we think and feel today, that verse reads:

> Instead of worrying, pray. Let petitions and praises shape your worries into prayers, letting God know your concerns. Before you know it, a sense of God's wholeness, everything coming together for good, will come and settle you down. It's wonderful what happens when Christ displaces worry at the center of your life (MSG).

Instead of worrying, pray. That's our God-given prescription for anxiety. As soon as we pray and hand our situation to God, He promises His peace will cover us and that peace will guard our hearts and minds from becoming distressed. As He gives us peace, depending on our need, He then provides us with wisdom from Scripture and the Holy Spirit, or with people who can help us—such as doctors, nutritionists, friends, family, and others.

You may be thinking, *Well that's a little simplistic. Just pray and it will all go away?* But it's not about prayer and *poof*, the situation changes. It's about surrender to your Maker and believing His promise that you are not alone. You have a Helper.

If you and I have access, through prayer, to the Living God who can do all things, why do we still stress and fear the worst will happen? Why do we claim we believe God is good and in control but not live like it? The disconnect is in who we truly believe God is.

You and I can't love, trust, and be transformed by God if we don't truly *know* His character. If we rely on our own thoughts, imaginations, or experiences of who we believe God is, rather than trusting what His Word says about Him, then we make ourselves vulnerable to anxiety and fear. Yet as you get to know the true character of God, as described in His Word, it will transform how you process life. Everything will be funneled through the fact that He is *with* you, He is *for* you, and He has a *reason* for where you are. Your trust, then, is not in principles, or in theories, or in three-step formulas from Christian books. Your trust is in a Person—Jesus, who assures us He is *with* us and will never leave.

EXAMINING WHAT YOU BELIEVE

There really *should* be a difference between a woman who knows God and a woman who doesn't. There really *should* be a difference in the peace and anxiety levels as well as the mental and emotional health conditions of those who possess eternal life and hope and those who don't. I believe that difference comes down to how well we *know* the character of God and therefore how much we *trust* Him.

If you're struggling with trusting the character of God, I must ask: What are you believing about God that isn't true? That He's forgotten you? That He doesn't have time for you? Do you believe He's given up on you or that He won't enable or equip you for the task ahead? Are you concerned that He cannot — or will not — heal you? Are you resolved to believing He is distant and uninterested in the specific details of your life?

Perhaps you believe He expects you to get yourself out of any mess that you got yourself into. If you happen to believe the popular lie "God helps those who help themselves," the truth is that God helps those *who admit they can't* help themselves. He steps in when we stop our exhaustive and futile efforts and surrender our situation to Him.

Psalm 34:8 tells us, "Taste and see that the LORD is good; how blessed is the man [or woman] who takes refuge in Him!" Look at that verse again. We are instructed by the psalmist to *taste* and see that the Lord is good. *Try* His goodness. *Test* His faithfulness. *Experience* His comfort. Live it. Savor it. And your eyes will be opened, and you will *see* that He is good.

If you really believed that God is good, how might you live each day differently? Would you be as quick to worry about whatever went wrong? Would you fear the circumstances you or your loved ones face? Would you get anxious or stressed if it didn't appear God was doing something in response to your prayers?

I once heard it said that God will give you only what you would have asked for if you knew everything He knows.

He knows so well what we need and what we don't need. Can you rest in the assurance that He is a good and loving Father who knows what's best for you and that He is truly *with* you?

STOP IMAGINING THE FUTURE

As I was awaiting a biopsy last year, my brother, Dan — a military and FBI veteran whom I often describe as a godly Jack Ryan — was stateside from his overseas job and text messaged me:

How are you doing?

Are you keeping control of your thoughts and imagination
about the future?

Don't let your thoughts run wild.

I was in the middle of writing a chapter for this book when I
received his message. I wrote back:

My fear was intense after I saw that horrible image from
the ultrasound, but after giving it to God and asking for
His peace in return, I'm reminded that I'm still securely
in God's arms, experiencing peace and no fear.

Dan texted in return:

We are in a survival course right now and we just had a
lesson that taught that most of our fears are not reality;
we often create fear as we try to imagine the future.

Whoa.

We often *create* fear as we try to imagine the future.

While there is a healthy kind of fear that keeps us from doing
something that might harm us (like the fear of fire, or of falling from
a building, or of running into a busy street), unnecessary fear that
is not reality occurs when we let our imaginations run wild and we
fear future events that "might" happen.

As I was digesting my brother's words, he added a disclaimer that
the survival course was being taught by military special forces.

Of course it was!, I thought. It makes perfect sense that the *elimination of fear* is practical for soldiers so they can stay focused in certain situations during physical warfare and don't freeze up or become
incapacitated by imagining the worst that could happen.

Scripture tells us God has not given us a spirit of fear, but of power and love and self-discipline (2 Timothy 1:7). The element of self-discipline is key here. We're to not let our imaginations run wild. We're to capture our thoughts of what might happen and bring them under His control, rather than let them run loose into all sorts of imaginations of what *could* happen.

Immediately after Philippians 4:6-7 tells us not to worry about anything but to pray about everything and experience God's peace (rather than the fear of what might happen), the next two verses tell us what to dwell on—only what is true or real, right, pure, lovely, and praiseworthy (verse 8). We are *commanded* not to dwell on what hasn't happened or the worst that could happen. God wants us to stay present—in the now—with Him, not to run out ahead of Him into the future.

As you and I deal with feelings of uncertainty or disappointment, our wandering thoughts of the future—of *What if…?*—can make the difference between snuggling securely into the arms of our Savior or keeping Him at arm's length, feeling alone, and pulling out our hair.

I want to take the safe and secure route, don't you? Take captive your thoughts that run wild about what might happen. About who might abandon you. About whether the funds will come through. About anything you can't control. And leave it with the Only One who really *is* in control. He's also the Only One who can calm your fears and fill your heart with peace. After all, every single one of your *What if…?* thoughts is rendered powerless by the single truth that God is *with* you.*

UNDERSTANDING
THE GOD WHO IS WITH US

Reading about spiritual truths from writers who lived a century or more before us can help us maintain a biblical perspective on our

---

* If you struggle with surrendering control to God, see my book *Women on the Edge* (Eugene, OR: Harvest House, 2010).

never-changing God in this ever-changing culture. James Smith, who wrote during Civil War times and mentored many men in the Christian faith, including Abraham Lincoln, wrote:

> The Lord's people are all prone to fear; because they do not realize their relation to God, their interest in the promises of God, and that they are always in the presence of God. How graciously our God forbids our slavish fears, and encourages confidence in Himself!... Beloved, leave anxiety, distrust, and slavish fear, to the poor, godless worldling; but trust thou in the living God: always, and everywhere. Hope in God; wait upon God; expect from God; follow hard after God: and all you want will be given, and all that would injure you will be frustrated. Be not afraid, only believe; Jesus is with thee, and will preserve, bless, and keep thee; therefore, "FEAR THOU NOT."[4]

So many books have been written on understanding our identity in Christ so we won't be anxious. So many talks have been given on seeing ourselves through God's eyes so we will live more confidently. But perhaps if we get our eyes off *ourselves* and our circumstances and insecurities and look to *Him* and Who His Word says He is, that might convince us of *Who* is *with us* and that He is capable of anything.

I mentioned to you at the beginning of this chapter that I started to feel lonely and anxious when I got a call from my doctor. I had forgotten, in the moment, *Who* God is. He is my Creator, Redeemer, Sustainer, and Helper. He is the Great Physician Who is always with me and knows exactly what's going on in my body. He is the One Who has an eternal purpose for those He loves. Don't forget *Who* He is.

God's Twofold Purpose for Us

When Jesus was asked which of God's commandments was the greatest, He said,

> "You shall love the Lord your God with all your heart, and with all your soul, and with all your mind." This is the great and foremost commandment. The second is like it, "You shall love your neighbor as yourself" (Matthew 22:37-39).

Jesus' summary of God's entire law into two commandments was also His summary of our purpose for existing. He was essentially telling us:

- Love God with everything you are and everything you have.

- Love others as much as you already love yourself. (More on this in chapter 7.)

How God Helps Us

There are at least three ways God helps us live out our twofold purpose to love Him with all our heart, soul, and mind, and to love others as ourselves:

- Through His divine provision and intervention in our lives[5]

- Through the power of His Word and prayer

- Through the people He places in our lives

However, when you and I try to find our purpose and alleviate our anxiety through a romantic relationship, a career, hobbies, achievements, children, grandchildren, or even one big "mission for God," we eventually find ourselves feeling lonely and unfulfilled because nothing and no one but God can fill that deep chasm in our hearts—that soul hole that longs for purpose, unconditional love, and eternal hope. Even if we try to alleviate our anxiety through meditation, rest, and self-care, we will still come up short. Our soul cries out for connection with our Maker and with those He has placed in our lives to minister to us.

The songwriters of Scripture knew this well. In Psalm 73:25-26, Asaph wrote these words, perhaps during a time of loneliness:

> Whom have I in heaven but You?
> And besides You, I desire nothing on earth.
> My flesh and my heart may fail,
> but God is the strength of my heart and my
> portion forever (NASB 1995).

I have related to those words during some of my loneliest times as a woman, wife, and mom. Many times, a mere *acknowledgment* that God is all we have and *all we want* is the first step toward losing the loneliness that occurs when we're outside the realm of an intimate relationship with Him. As we grow closer to Him, He can then help us trust any people He happens to bring into our lives, and sometimes they will help us grow closer to Him too.

WHY WE STILL STRUGGLE

If you and I are convinced God really is *with* us, and He is capable of handling all that concerns us, why do we still become anxious and fearful and experience loneliness? With all the biblical evidence for what we mean to our Creator God and all that He has given us, promised us, and entrusted us with, why do we not live like this is our identity and inheritance?

There are times when we can get caught up in our circumstances and forget Who God is, what He's capable of, and how much He has us on His mind. I believe that might be the reason so many of us experience an anxious mindset—we have yet to apply what we know about God to our real-life situations and remember that He is absolutely capable of getting us through whatever we face minute by minute, day by day.

DON'T FORGET WHO IS WITH YOU

Lest you think I'm writing this from a position of having learned it all, God recently made me aware of how anxious I can become when I forget Who is with me.

I was preparing for a five-day trip to North Africa with my husband (Hugh) and daughter (Dana), where we would tour the Sahara Desert, see locations where *Star Wars* and *Raiders of the Lost Ark* were filmed, and experience life on the other side of the world. Hugh and Dana were beyond excited for the adventure that was ahead of us. But the closer we got to taking our trip, the more fearful I became.

The night before we left, I slept very little. The impending 14-hour flight, the different foods, the lack of sanitation in some areas, and all the variables of risk for three light-skinned Americans who would stand out in a predominantly Muslim country seemed too much to fathom.

But then a calm overcame me as I remembered who was going to be there with us.

A Desert Storm war veteran and former FBI analyst who now works as a risk management consultant for an overseas company was meeting us there. He was familiar with the territory we'd be visiting. And keeping Americans safe was his expertise. I had forgotten I was going with my brother, Dan, the one I referred to earlier as my "godly Jack Ryan."

The moment we arrived, Dan was there to greet us. He gave us the ground rules of what we needed to do to be safe. He advised us to follow his lead as he walked ahead of us, listen for his cues or code words if he sensed we were in any possible danger, and be ready for a sudden change of plans if he deemed it necessary. As long as we kept our eyes on him, heeded his warnings, and remained flexible, we would be safe.

If I had not listened to my brother and followed his lead, I would've literally fallen in several places where the infrastructure wasn't secure (safety codes are nonexistent in that country) or been hit by numerous passing vehicles while crossing streets (traffic rules don't exist there either). Yet I was safe, cared for, and even treated like royalty at times because I was with and paid attention to our guide. (And by the way, I absolutely can't wait to return to North Africa—as long as my brother goes with us.)

As safe as I felt while following my brother, he is not all-knowing. He was aware of the variables and possible threats, but he is still human and fallible, and anything still could have taken him—and us—by surprise. Dan was constantly on alert, but ultimately, God was our protector.

Dear friend, can your anxiety and mine be a result of forgetting Who is *with* us on this journey in life?

We have an all-knowing, all-powerful Guide who not only knows the territory, but has gone before us into all things. As we follow our Savior, He knows exactly what's coming and how to steer us on the right path. He is prepared for everything and has already solved every problem we may encounter. You and I are so much more secure under the protection of our all-knowing, ever-present God than with anyone else this side of heaven who offers us security.

The opposite of anxiety is *confidence in the person and presence of God.* As long as we keep our eyes on Jesus, follow His lead, and heed His warnings, we are safer and more secure than we can possibly be on our own.

Don't ever forget *Who* is with you. He can get you securely through whatever lies ahead.

WHERE JOY IS FOUND

Without a close relationship with God, there can be no peace or joy. There can be no sense of support. There can be no calm or confidence. And when we have solid relationships with other followers of Jesus, we can have daily reminders that He is with us, supportive strength when we start to feel weak, and helpful encouragement when the enemy tries to make us believe we are alone. To the contrary, joy is absent when sin has us avoiding God—or His people. Anytime we allow sin or doubt to come between us and God, we forfeit peace and joy.

Psalm 16:11 assures us *in His presence* there is *fullness* of joy.

We lose our contentment and joy when we're in sin, when we're looking somewhere other than to God for our fulfillment, when we're not in God's Word regularly, or when we don't have mature believers around to help us grow in our faith.

Philippians 1:6 says we are each a work in progress, but it's a *joyful* progress when we're gradually growing and moving forward day by day as an obedient follower of Jesus. If you are truly abiding in God and in His Word, you will experience His peace and His joy, and you will rest assured you are not alone.

If you are truly abiding in God and in His Word,
you will experience His peace and His joy, and
you will rest assured you are not alone.

ADOPT A JESUS-ONLY MINDSET

Before I close out this chapter, I must make the point that loneliness also occurs when we're convinced we must have a man in our lives. Right now, you might be thinking: *That's easy for you to say,*

Cindi. You've been married for more than 35 years. Yes, I have, and I can attest to the fact that being married—or simply having a man in one's life—is not the cure for loneliness. Not only have I experienced that God alone satisfies, but as a pastor's wife, former women's ministry director, and someone who has mentored single and married women for the past four decades, I've heard the firsthand accounts of what women struggle with and never has a woman said (after at least one year of marriage), "I am no longer lonely now that I'm married." When the honeymoon wears off, so does the fantasy that having a husband will fill you up completely and eliminate loneliness altogether.

As I've been saying in my books and at my conferences for the past 25 years, only God satisfies. It's when we want God *plus* a husband, God *plus* a career, God *plus* children, God *plus* financial security, God *plus* notoriety, and so on that we find ourselves anxious, lonely, and sometimes depressed. For that reason, I encourage you to go at least 21 days this month with a Jesus-only mindset. (It is believed that after 21 days of repetitive thought or actions, a habit is formed.)

Yes, we also need others in our lives (which I'll get to in the second and third sections of this book), but we must *start* with the foundational concept that it is God alone who can satisfy us. When we truly seek and depend on Him alone, we won't want to put someone or something else ahead of Him. As imperfect humans we naturally desire more, so we must settle the more by fully believing *He is enough.*

Jesus gave us the secret for not only having our material needs met, but for finding fulfillment and easing our anxieties as well. He said,

> Seek first His kingdom and His righteousness, and all these
> things will be added to you (Matthew 6:33 NASB 1995).

Jesus was saying "Desire Me first, and I'll make sure you have all you need"—all the calm, all the contentment, all the confidence, all the companionship. I've seen many times—in my own life and in the lives of women I've mentored—that God, in His goodness, will often give so much of what we *want*, too, when we look to Him to provide only what we need. As we desire Jesus alone, we become content with the blessings He chooses to give, and we become more aware of His goodness everywhere we look.

YOU CAN DO THIS

Are you ever on your own when it comes to uncertainty, anxiety, or fear? Absolutely not. The God who wants your communion is *with* you, and He wants your life to reflect a steady awareness of His provision, His protection, and His presence. Be a conduit through which He can show the world how strong and capable He is. Big responsibility? Yes. Tremendous privilege? You bet. Doable? Absolutely—with His strength and grace.

You can do *all* things through Him who is standing by to strengthen you. You are not alone, my sister. You do not have to continue feeling uncertain, anxious, or lonely. You are a woman through whom God can do amazing things.

BEING INTENTIONAL

By getting into God's Word and learning more about His character, we can be assured that He is with us and will help us navigate and overcome feelings of loneliness and anxiety.

1. Read Psalm 139. Below, record what the following verses say about the God who is with you:

   Verses 1-2:

   Verse 4:

   Verses 8-10:

   Verses 13-14:

   Verse 16:

Verses 17-18:

Consider what you learned from these verses about God's intimate knowledge of you. How can this help you process life differently?

In the space below, write a prayerful response to God's heart for you (as expressed in Psalm 139):

2. What causes you to worry and start imagining what might happen in the future?

3. What one or two verses come to your mind that could help you when you begin to imagine the future? Write your favorite one below. (If you don't have one already, this is a good time to find one and write it out.)

Consider committing this verse (or these verses) to memory so it is fresh in your mind the next time fear or worry bombard you.

4. Read Psalm 73:25-26. What would it take for the psalmist's words to be your own?

5. John 1:1 tells us Jesus *is* the Word. How can you embrace Jesus the Word as closely as you'd like to embrace Jesus the Person? Write your thoughts or draw a picture to express your heart in the space below.

A CHALLENGE TO HELP YOU GROW

Consider adopting a Jesus-only mindset for the next 21 days by doing the following:

- Read a chapter in the Gospel of John each day.

- Ask Jesus, before and after your reading, to help you long for Him above anything or anyone else.

- Recite this prayer in Psalm 73:25 and make it your own:

  Whom have I in heaven but You?
  And besides You, I desire nothing on earth.

- Each time you start to worry or fret, say this out loud as a reminder of Who is in control of everything that comes your way: "God is *with* me, He is *for* me, and there's a reason He has me here."

CHAPTER 2

THE LONELINESS OF SHAME

Realizing Who Is *for* You

*Those who enter into Christ's being-here-for-us no longer
have to live under a continuous, low-lying black cloud.*

ROMANS 8:1 (MSG)

Shame.

We all have felt it. It either clings to us constantly, haunts us at certain times, or tries to nudge its way into our minds when we remember something that hurt us or that we did to hurt someone else.

Maybe you were teased about your body or shamed for something you said when you were younger. Or perhaps you were carelessly labeled by a parent or cruelly taunted by a bully in middle school and you've let those stinging words define you. Maybe you can't forgive yourself for something you've done, or your shame was thrust on you from someone else and what they did to you.

Scientific American magazine defines shame as "the uncomfortable sensation we feel in the pit of our stomach when it seems we have no safe haven from the judging gaze of others. It makes us feel small and bad about ourselves and wish we could vanish." (Do you see how social media has contributed to opportunities for others to judge us and make us feel small? Add to that element our post-pandemic isolation tendencies and shame has nowhere to go but inward, continuing to deteriorate our souls and exacerbate the new loneliness we are feeling.)

The article continued, "Although shame is a universal emotion, how it affects mental health and behavior is not self-evident."[1]

Yes, shame is a universal emotion. And it was present in your life and mine before we met the healing power of the cross. But once we are truly in Christ Jesus, shame never needs to take residence again in our hearts or minds. (Notice I didn't say *once we never sin again*.) When we are *in relationship with Christ Jesus*, trusting in His work on the cross to cover our sin nature, Jesus defends us (and our unchanging position in Him) before the throne of God.[2] Jesus defends us day and night from the accusations of Satan, our enemy and chief accuser who wants nothing more than for us to keep living in shame and not experience the joy and freedom that comes through a relationship with Christ.

Scripture tells us, "If God is for us, who is against us?" (Romans 8:31).

Friend, in what Jesus did for us, you and I truly have a "safe haven from the judging gaze of others." God is not only *with* us. He is *for* us.

OUR COMPASSIONATE DEFENDER

In the Bible, we read many times about that "judging gaze of others." And nearly every time, Jesus sets the judgmental crowd straight, calling out their own sin when they're trying to shame others. In John 8, we are told that the religious leaders brought a woman to Jesus and threw her at His feet, saying:

> "Teacher, this woman has been caught in the very act of committing adultery. Now in the Law, Moses commanded

us to stone such women; what then do You say?" Now they were saying this to test Him, so that they might have grounds for accusing Him. But Jesus stooped down and with His finger wrote on the ground (verses 4-6).

Some scholars believe Jesus was writing out the Ten Commandments in the dirt, or perhaps listing the sins of the men in that circle who were accusing the woman. Jesus might have even been writing the names of the men who had also sinned with that woman, or who had committed adultery with someone else. (Notice they didn't bring before Jesus the man who was "caught in the very act" with her. This smells of a setup, doesn't it?)

Scripture continues:

> When they persisted in asking Him, He straightened up and said to them, "He who is without sin among you, let him be the first to throw a stone at her." And again He stooped down and wrote on the ground. Now when they heard this, they began leaving, one by one, beginning with the older ones, and He was left alone, and the woman where she was, in the center of the courtyard. And straightening up, Jesus said to her, "Woman, where are they? Did no one condemn you?" She said, "No one, Lord." And Jesus said, "I do not condemn you, either. Go. From now on do not sin any longer" (verses 7-11).

Jesus had every right to judge this woman, but He showed compassion on her instead. How much more compassion will He have for you when you've confessed your sin to Him? If you are trusting in Jesus as your Savior, you don't need to fear His judgment for something you've done in the past. Nor do you need to carry the shame any longer (1 John 1:9; 2 Corinthians 5:17).

GOD'S MERCY NULLIFIES SHAME

Scripture tells us another story in Luke 7 of a sinful woman, a prostitute, who crashed a dinner party attended by Jesus and some religious leaders. She may have been seeking to rid herself of guilt and shame.

> Just then a woman of the village, the town harlot, having learned that Jesus was a guest in the home of the Pharisee, came with a bottle of very expensive perfume and stood at his feet, weeping, raining tears on his feet. Letting down her hair, she dried his feet, kissed them, and anointed them with the perfume. When the Pharisee who had invited him saw this, he said to himself, "If this man was the prophet I thought he was, he would have known what kind of woman this is who is falling all over him" (verses 37-39 MSG).

Although the Pharisee, whose name was Simon, didn't speak those thoughts aloud, Jesus heard them anyway and saw the men's judgmental hearts against this woman who was surrendering her all. Jesus called out their hypocritical piety by telling a parable of two people and the huge differences in debt that they were forgiven. He asked which one would be more grateful for the forgiveness of their debt, and Simon said, "I suppose the one who was forgiven the most" (verse 43 MSG). Jesus' point was that when one has been forgiven much, they tend to love much.

> Then turning to the woman, but speaking to Simon, [Jesus] said, "Do you see this woman? I came to your home; you provided no water for my feet, but she rained tears on my feet and dried them with her hair. You gave me no greeting, but from the time I arrived she hasn't quit kissing my feet. You provided nothing for freshening up,

but she has soothed my feet with perfume. Impressive, isn't it? She was forgiven many, many sins, and so she is very, very grateful. If the forgiveness is minimal, the gratitude is minimal."

Then he spoke to her: "I forgive your sins."

That set the dinner guests talking behind his back: "Who does he think he is, forgiving sins!"

He ignored them and said to the woman, "Your faith has saved you. Go in peace" (verses 44-50 MSG).

OUR SHAME AND BROKENNESS

Why are you and I so moved by the stories of Jesus' tenderness and compassion toward women who were in shame? Could it be that we sometimes feel it is *our* story? Is it because we long to pour our tears on the literal feet of Jesus, and to hear His compassionate words that we are forgiven? Scripture tells us we all have sinned and fallen short of His glory (Romans 3:23). If you have repented of your sin condition and given your life to Christ, chances are you still feel the shame of your actions or lifestyle *before* entering that saving relationship with Jesus. But, dear one, if you have sincerely repented of the sin in your life, these stories aren't about you any longer. Sin—which naturally produces shame—was a disease you were born with, a condition you were redeemed of when you received Jesus as your Savior.

Our repentance from sin is what was needed in order to accept the free gift of salvation offered from Christ. But what about the sins we commit after becoming a believer? The confession of those sins to God—and one another—is what restores our fellowship with God, Who doesn't see us as shameful anymore, no matter what we've done (1 John 1:9). That shameful state died with Jesus on the cross. You live before Him now as a *new creation*, one who no longer carries shame, but is covered by the pure cleansing blood of Jesus and bears a new name: redeemed one in Christ.

If you still struggle with shame over sins from before you became a Christian, you can let go of that shame. Christ has forgiven you, and His atoning death on the cross redeems you from *all* sin — past, present, and future — and sets you free from sin's eternal consequences.

After the woman in Luke 7 repented of her sin (as evidenced by her tears and love for the Lord), Jesus set her free. She was forgiven, redeemed, a new woman. She never needed to bear any type of shame again. God has set you free from shame too. On the cross, God treated Jesus as if He had lived your life so He can now treat you as if you had lived *His*. That's a position before God that you and I didn't earn on our own. And it's a position before Him that we can do nothing to change. Why, then, would we allow ourselves to revisit the steam room of shame and let that shame soak into our pores and impact how we live?

WHY SHAME HAPPENS

You are not fully to blame for continuing to wear shame when you've been set free of it as a new person in Christ. There may be someone else dictating your wardrobe — someone who keeps suggesting you wear those dirty rags of shame. Satan is that someone who tries to convince you that you wouldn't look good wearing anything else. The Bible calls Satan "the one who accuses [us] before our God day and night" (Revelation 12:10). He is a liar, a master of deception who comes to steal, kill, and destroy (John 10:10). And Satan does that by trying to get us to ignore the beautiful, white "robe of righteousness" that Scripture says Jesus has covered us with (Isaiah 61:10). As Satan keeps trying to cover us with our old coat of shame, I must ask: Why would you and I wear a filthy, ragged, heavy coat in the midst of Jesus' warmth and light, when we could wear that robe of white?

Although Jesus removed our shame at the cross and no longer sees it anywhere on us, it can be difficult to believe it's completely gone when we remember what we were once ashamed of. But God, who is incapable of forgetting *anything*, has fully chosen to forget just *one* thing—our sin, when we've repented of it and allowed Him to cover it through His Son's death at Calvary.

In Psalm 103:12, we are assured of this:

> As far as the east is from the west,
> so far has He removed our wrongdoings from us.

In addition, God spoke through the prophet Isaiah, "I, I alone, am the one who wipes out your wrongdoings for My own sake, and I will not remember your sins" (43:25).

Now if you and I could forget our past sins as God does, we could have far better relationships with God and those around us. Yet as is true with most aspects of the Christian walk, faith is required to take God at His Word. Faith is required to believe our shame and past sins are truly gone, and we can live fulfilling lives with God and others.

SHAME IS NOTHING NEW

While shame has existed ever since sin came into our world, I believe the loneliness of shame is even more prevalent today because of the public opinion platform that exists on the internet, allowing anyone to shame or bully someone else on social media or other sites where public comments are allowed. While it used to be that only celebrities or people who suddenly had a spotlight thrust upon them could be publicly shamed, it is now possible for anyone with an online presence to be the target of insults, slurring remarks, or outright bullying, all which can add to our level of personal shame and loneliness. Sometimes careless, hurtful comments from others can trigger memories or insecurities within us, and we can tend to believe those comments and opinions and allow them to penetrate our hearts. And whereas someone used to have the opportunity to shame us only through a personal comment or a prank phone call, now it's as easy as looking us up online and sending a snarky email, or posting something reckless and hurtful on one of our social posts.

HOW SHAME IMPACTS
OUR RELATIONSHIPS

When you and I see ourselves as shameful, whether it is because of our own past actions or what someone has said about us, others sense our wounds and that impenetrable wall we erect around us, and it can repel them from wanting to be around us. Shame begets shame. Why do we want to be around positive people rather than cynical or negative people? Often, we are hoping their positivity will rub off on us, right? Why do we tend to avoid people who complain constantly? Because we don't want them to bring us down or trigger a critical spirit in us as well. Why do others not want to be around you or me when we are wearing unnecessary shame? Because it may remind them of theirs...and theirs is often too heavy to deal with, let alone having to deal with ours too. That's why we need to give our burden of shame to the Only One who can remove it from us and allow us to start over. Imagine life—and relationships with others—in which shame has no role. Sounds like heaven on earth, doesn't it? And yet it's your present reality when you understand Who has forgiven you, Who is ultimately *for* you, and Who has permanently covered your shame.

THE DIFFERENCE BETWEEN SHAME
AND GOD'S CONVICTION OF SIN

Simply put, shame is from us (or from the enemy of our souls). It's an accusing voice, a blaming and condemning voice, a derogatory voice that says, "You're a failure. You're a loser. You're worthless. You're a horrible person to do that and still call yourself a Christian." Do you hear how stinging and biting that voice can be? Trust me, my friend, that inner voice is not the voice of God's Holy Spirit.

When God's Spirit convicts us of sin, He does not do so in a demeaning way. God's voice doesn't attack who we *are*, it sheds light on what we've *done* that is displeasing to Him. He convicts our hearts of our sinful thoughts and actions with an eye toward restoring our unity with Him. God's motivation is love and a restored relationship, not judgment, condemnation, or revenge (Romans 8:1). There is a reason Jesus referred to the Holy Spirit—who indwells every believer—as our *Comforter* and *Counselor,* not our condemner. Satan is the *accuser* and *deceiver,* so don't ever get his voice mixed up with the tender voice of the Spirit, who is your *Advocate* and *Defender.*

When Jesus saved us, God rewrote our identity from sinner to saint. And shame certainly accompanied that old description of us as a sinner. But *saint* is now God's definition of us, even though, at times, our thoughts and actions lapse into sin. That new identity as saint is based on *who we are now* because of what *He* did for us, not because of anything we do or fail to do.[3]

When you and I continue to sin after we've been saved, we can feel the loneliness of shame, but that is because the Holy Spirit is doing His convicting work in us. When we are in relationship with God and living in sin too, God's Spirit convicts our hearts so that we will confess (admit and own up to) that sin and return to a right relationship with Him. But God's conviction on our hearts is often gentle and is meant to soften our hearts toward repentance. But if we persist in our sin, we end up hardening our hearts, which makes us deaf to the Spirit's gentle voice.

Society will tell us anytime we feel badly about something, that's shame, and we should reject that feeling. But we never want to shut out the Holy Spirit's gentle conviction on our hearts. If anytime we feel shame with good reason and we attempt to shut it out, or if a mature believer confronts us in love about sin and we refuse to listen because we believe they are shaming us, we could be refusing the refining work God's Holy Spirit wants to do in us.

David prayed in Psalm 139:23-24:

> Search me, God, and know my heart;
> put me to the test and know my anxious thoughts;
> and see if there is any hurtful way in me,
> and lead me in the everlasting way.

I have found it spiritually healthy to invite God's Holy Spirit to examine my heart frequently, as David did in his song, and reveal to me ways I might be hurting the heart of God. That keeps me from defining any kind of criticism or helpful correction as "shaming," and it prevents me from developing a prideful heart that thinks I can do no wrong. However, if I get too introspective and focus too much on myself and my lack or desire for purity, it can lead to a sense of pride as well. Let me explain.

Letting God examine our hearts and motives is good. Blaming ourselves for everything that goes wrong is destructive. Continual self-blame causes us to put aside Christ's garment of righteousness that He placed upon us when He exchanged our guilt and shame for His righteousness, and slip back into the old, worn-out cloak of shame.

Although you and I want to be sensitive to God's gentle conviction on our hearts, we also need to extend grace to ourselves as God does. Sometimes the very act of punishing ourselves with guilt and shame results from a prideful spirit that thinks, *I can't believe I would do something like that. I'm so ashamed of myself.* When it comes to your heart and behavior, be aware of your vulnerability to sin. Except for the grace of God, you and I are capable of any sin. Therefore, be humble and thankful for God's grace, but don't slip into a prideful state that refuses to believe you could sink to a certain low or disappoint God in some way. And don't grovel by shaming yourself for it either. Shame is another way we end up focusing on self. Recognizing God's grace and forgiveness helps us to stay focused on Him.

THAT ACCUSING INNER VOICE

I mentioned earlier that feelings of shame can come from Satan. But sometimes Satan isn't even involved. People who are blind to their own sins are pretty good at shaming others, and we happen to be especially critical of ourselves. Could your shame be coming from a lie someone once told you or a lie your own inner critic keeps repeating? Shame often sounds the opposite of what you'll read in God's Word. For example:

- Shame condemns. God's Word reassures us there is *no condemnation* in Christ Jesus (Romans 8:1).

- Shame tells us we are wrecked, damaged, and beyond repair. God's Word tells us we are a *new creation* in Christ Jesus (2 Corinthians 5:17).

- Shame tells us we will never amount to anything in God's eyes or anyone else's. God's Word tells us we are *loved* with an everlasting love (Jeremiah 31:3) and we are His *masterpiece* (Ephesians 2:10 NLT).

- Shame tells us we have exhausted our chances. God's Word tells us His grace abounds and we are *as forgiven as God is rich* (Ephesians 1:7).

TALK IT THROUGH
WITH ANOTHER BELIEVER

When we are isolated from others, or we are alone in our thoughts, the enemy can have a heyday with us — especially if we're not telling someone how we're feeling and listening to their words of wisdom about where our shameful feelings are coming from.

Alexa, a young wife and mom who strives to have a closer walk with Jesus, confided in me about what women her age struggle with: "We tend to feel alone in our situations only to later realize, when we actually open up about them, that a lot of us are struggling with those same thoughts and feelings."

Think about Alexa's words. There is a comforting reassurance that comes from knowing you and I are not alone in what we feel and experience. We can find it beneficial to talk about those feelings with another believer who is grounded in God's Word and who can help us discern what is bringing on those shameful feelings.

Alexa said, "I also feel like I can tend to make a bigger deal of things than they actually are, but I'm constantly reminding myself that while my feelings are real, they are not always true."

Being grounded in God's Word can help us recognize the truth and separate our feelings from the facts. But if we're trying to do that on our own, we can miss the help God designed the body of believers to be for us when we're struggling.

IDENTIFYING THE TRUTH

I mentioned in chapter 1 that Philippians 4:8 tells us to think on whatever is true, honorable, and right. Your feelings of shame are *not* true if you are in Christ Jesus. The secret to ridding your mind and memory of shame is to believe what God's Word says. First John 4:4 assures us "greater is He who is in you [the Holy Spirit] than he who is in the world [Satan]." God's Holy Spirit gives you the faith to believe the truth and the power to resist the enemy's lies. Here are the basics — the ABCs of how you can keep the truth foremost in your mind when shame tries to creep back in.

A — *Acknowledge that shame is gone.* Again, Psalm 103:12 assures us that as far as the east is from the west, so far has He removed our wrongdoings (and that includes our guilt and shame) from us. Memorize this short verse so that you can let this truth really sink in.

B— *Believe you're truly free.* Romans 8:1 assures us that God no longer holds any of your sin against you. Believe it. To not believe it is to call God a liar.

C— *Claim your new identity in Christ.* Consider reading through the first chapter of Ephesians every morning for a month until you begin to see yourself the way the chapter describes you. That chapter defines who you are in Christ—not in the future, not until the next time you sin, but right now, today, and always. You may also want to memorize 2 Corinthians 5:17: "If anyone is in Christ, this person is a new creation; the old things passed away; behold, new things have come." I love the word "behold" in that verse. It means "look—be amazed, how incredible the newness that has come."

In *The Message*—a paraphrase based on the original Greek and Hebrew into idiomatic English which represents the way we think and feel today—that passage, along with the following verse, reads like this:

> Now we look inside, and what we see is that anyone united with the Messiah gets a fresh start, is created new. The old life is gone; a new life emerges! Look at it! All this comes from the God who settled the relationship between us and him, and then called us to settle our relationships with each other.

Wow! In light of that passage, we begin to understand how our newness—and no longer identifying ourselves with our past shame—can help us in our relationships and reconciliation with others. When you and I are still living in the shame of our past, we will see others—and their actions toward us—through the lens of our wounds. And that can trigger us to respond hurtfully toward them or ourselves. But God has made us new—people who no longer bear shame and who no longer need to be triggered by our past—so that we can be equipped to love and serve others as He intended.

Embrace that shame-free existence, my sister in Christ! It's yours. It's who you really are.

Remember when I told you earlier that Satan wants to convince you that you won't look good wearing anything else but a cloak of shame? Scripture tells us Jesus has already set aside garments of white for you to wear, symbolizing your purity and righteousness in His eyes. He has for you a robe of righteousness (Isaiah 61:10), as if you'd never sinned at all. As if you had lived *His* life, not yours. That is your appropriate clothing now. Receive it, wear it, and let His purity and righteousness become your new identity. When you do, shame has no body or mind to cling to…it falls to the ground and is taken out with the trash.

Ruth Chou Simons said it so eloquently in her book *Pilgrim*: "When we see ourselves as God sees us, through the lens of grace, we will realize we no longer need to make ourselves right through attempts at worthiness. We can walk in righteousness because God has made us right with Him."[4]

WHEN LOVE SPEAKS
LOUDER THAN SHAME

During the past couple of years, I've had some precious talks with my older sister, Kristi, about some regretted behavior toward my siblings during childhood. I didn't realize it, but I was still holding on to feelings of guilt and shame about looking out for myself and not my sister and younger brother. At times, I have unknowingly let that define who I am, when I'm feeling that God might be disappointed in me.

Every time I have opened up to Kristi about something I was ashamed of in my youth, her response has been like a soothing salve being poured over a long-irritated wound. One time I told her about an incident and asked, "Why didn't I do what you would have done? You were always looking after our little brother. Why was I so selfish?"

Kristi's love spoke louder than my shame. "Can you let that little girl off the hook for not knowing any better at the time?" she asked gently. "Would you have scolded your own daughter for what you believe you needed scolding for?"

When she put the scenario into the context of a mother, I had compassion on the child I was so long ago. I never would have scolded my daughter for failing to do something because she was afraid of the repercussions. I would have used it as an opportunity for a gentle teaching moment that God can give us confidence, help us when we're scared, and cleanse and comfort our hearts when we are truly sorry for anything we've done.

God's Word tells us, "If you, despite being evil, know how to give good gifts to your children, how much more will your Father who is in heaven give good things to those who ask Him!" (Matthew 7:11).

That conversation with Kristi helped me discern my compassionate heavenly Father's heart toward me as a child too, instead of continuing to define myself as selfish and uncompassionate because of my actions toward my siblings when I was younger. When God says we are a new creation, He means completely. We are set free and redeemed from every mistake or selfish attitude or perspective we've ever had. Our relationship with God today is defined by our new creation life instead of our old sinful ways.

Every time I talk with Kristi about dysfunction from our childhood or regrets I had while growing up, I am exposed to another layer of self-inflicted shame that's been clinging to me. And I'm reminded once again that it has no truth to it, and I have been set free.

Our relationship with God today is defined by our
new creation life instead of our old sinful ways.

FIND SOMEONE TO SHARE IT WITH

Who can you talk to when you struggle with feelings of shame? Do you have someone who will remind you of the truths of God's Word and help you distinguish between the lies of the accuser and the tender whispers from your Advocate? At first, to talk about our shame with others can feel risky, but it can be so freeing.

Instead of remaining in an isolated state when it comes to feelings of shame and consulting the advice found on your device, reach out to someone you trust who can help you. You need a sister (in Christ) who will remind you that Jesus has removed your shame. Start praying now about who that friend is or whom you can approach to be that friend. Later in this book, I'll share ideas for how to find her if she's not already in your life. Surrounding yourself with others who are grounded in God's Word is another step forward and away from the new loneliness that will otherwise hold you down.

BEING INTENTIONAL

1. When you see or hear the word *shame*, what images or "memory reels" go through your mind? Tell God, in a prayer journal or in the space below, the things you need to no longer think about. (He's already forgiven you for them, but by telling Him, or writing them down, you are releasing them to Him again and trusting Him to remove them from you.)

2. Read Psalm 103. Highlight the verses in that psalm that particularly resonate with you. Now record in the space below which of those verses you need to remember or return to often. (For example, verses 3-4, 11-13, and so on.)

3. Read Romans 12:2. What is one way you can renew your mind so you are more focused on God's gentle conviction on your heart than the shame-inducing words of the enemy?

4. Read 2 Corinthians 5:17. In the space below, write a description (or draw a picture) of what a new creation looks like.

How can you begin to live like the "old things [have] passed away" and "new things have come"?

5. Read Romans 8:31-39. Record the key principles of what God has done or will do for you, based on this passage.

Based on what you just read in Romans 8:31-39, prayerfully reflect on your Advocate and Defender. Write a short prayer below, thanking Jesus for what He did on the cross to cover your shame.

A CHALLENGE TO HELP YOU GROW

Write Psalm 103:12 below and say it at least once every morning this week. Chances are good you'll have it committed to memory within three to five days. It will help you remember that your shame is covered, and the Holy Spirit is your Comforter, not your condemner.

For more on stepping out of shame and into a more trusting relationship with the God who has forgiven you, see my book *When a Woman Overcomes Life's Hurts* (use coupon code TNL5 to save $5 on that book when ordered from my website store www.StrengthForTheSoul.com).

CHAPTER 3

THE LONELINESS OF SUFFERING AND LOSS

Understanding Why You're Here

*In every trouble, remember, God is now especially
present; He is with you to hear your prayer, increase your
strength, direct your way, and make you a conqueror.*[1]

JAMES SMITH

Alyssa has known suffering from the time she was a child. But she readily admits it is what made her who she is today and allows her to help others who are struggling.

Mental illness was prevalent in Alyssa's family, showing up in obsessive-compulsive disorder (OCD) tendencies, depression, and borderline personality disorder among various family members. At four-and-a-half years old, Alyssa lost her teenage brother, who took his life while he was institutionalized. Without an ability to cope with the trauma, Alyssa started exhibiting OCD behavior at age seven, and by the time she was eleven, she was institutionalized for the next six years.

"The OCD I experienced grew so bad it became debilitating," she said. At first, she received acute hospitalization in a children's psychiatric ward, then in outpatient care, then in a state hospital and residential care.

"When I was in the residential facility, I'd come home on weekends and go to church and youth group, and that helped me a lot," Alyssa said. Attending a church youth group helped her form a foundation of faith — she learned that God existed and He could help her.

"I had religion back then, as I was growing up, but not a relationship with Christ," Alyssa said. Church helped to provide structure for her life, but as she grew older, she realized her need for a personal relationship with the Savior.

The key to Alyssa's mental and spiritual healing was realizing life wasn't about following rules or a religious system, but rather, about following, loving, and serving a Person — Jesus. After she entered into a relationship with God, she was better able to deal with feelings of loneliness and isolation, which had intensified during her treatment for mental illness.

WHEN LOSS SETS IN

Alyssa had moved from the East Coast to Southern California to continue working for a Home Depot store. She began attending a large church and volunteering for its special-needs ministry. She originally wanted to work with emotionally disturbed children. But through her volunteer work she gained a passion for working with autistic individuals. She sensed God leading her to quit her career job with Home Depot and start moving toward helping children with special needs.

At that point, Alyssa had seven years invested with Home Depot, a lucrative salary, a 401(k), quarterly bonuses, and full-time health benefits. But it wasn't her passion. She felt God calling her to more.

Alyssa gave up her apartment, sold nearly everything she owned, moved in to a small room she rented where she had no privacy, and took three part-time jobs in the field she was interested in so she could pursue her desire to become a behavioral analyst. The part-time jobs brought in far less income, but she knew she was doing what she was called to do, so she made the sacrifices and trusted God to provide.

"I forfeited my whole life to quit my Home Depot management job and work those other jobs so I could do respite care, applied behavioral analysis (ABA) therapy, and be a behavioral intervention-ist at school," Alyssa said. Yet five months after leaving her lucrative job, she injured her knee. As a result, she had two knee surgeries over the next several months.

Because Alyssa needed time off for the surgeries, and because her places of employment could no longer provide her the disability access she required as she was recovering, she lost all three of her income-producing jobs.

"I worked so hard and had given up so much to pursue this call-ing," she said. "I felt this was God's will and God's work, and this was what He wanted me to do." Yet roadblock after roadblock and surgery after surgery, Alyssa became discouraged and wondered if she hadn't heard God's calling after all. Perhaps she wasn't supposed to be doing what she loved to do. She ended up being out of work for nearly two years and dealing with the loneliness that comes from confusion and disappointment.

SURRENDER IN THE SUFFERING

"I felt my life had been ripped away from me and I had lost my pur-pose," Alyssa said. "I wasn't angry at God; I simply asked Him to help me understand why." After her injury, she dove intently into the Bible's book of Job. "I remember praying that God would give me the kind of faith Job had when he lost everything and still trusted in Him."

As Alyssa continued to trust God with her circumstances, even though it didn't look like things were improving, God proved Him-self faithful.

"God brought the right people into my life through Bible Study Fellowship," Alyssa recalled. "Those Bible studies met midmorning and had I been working, I could not have attended." Through the meetings, she gained a deeper knowledge of God and His ways, and she began to understand what He might be doing through her circumstances.

Alyssa's injury—and the doors that closed as a result of it—helped her to see who she was apart from her pursuits or accomplishments, and Who God was in spite of all that was happening.

"I see now that His plans were so much greater than mine. But in the moment, I fell into a very deep depression." She then had to reach out to the resources available to help her grow her faith and trust in the Only One who was in control of her life.

"I realized what I'd been doing wrong. I had put my worth into those jobs—first with Home Depot, and then as a behavioral therapist. When I got hurt and couldn't work and help people, I kept saying, 'I lost my purpose.'"

But she realizes today it wasn't her purpose she lost. It was her perspective.

"I was looking at my job and saying, 'This is mine.' I was looking at all I had at the time and thinking, *This is mine.* Now, I realize *nothing* is mine." She realizes instead that she, and all she has, belongs to God.

"That's when my walk with God became so strong during my healing—when I felt I had lost everything, but then I realized it was never mine in the first place."

Upon realizing that everything she had was God's, Alyssa's sense of purpose and worth as a child and servant of God was renewed. She also discovered that the God Who had closed certain doors as a result of her injury was preparing her with new doors of opportunity—to know Him better, to be assured of her purpose, and to meet her husband.

GOD'S REDEMPTION

While Alyssa was beginning to see her worth from God's perspective—apart from what she did or didn't do—the Lord brought a godly man into her life. This happened right when she believed she might never find one.

"Before I met Wes, it was difficult to meet anybody," Alyssa said. "I was working three jobs and in grad school, was very busy, and just wasn't into dating.

"I thought about Abraham and Sarah's story. I wanted to be patient and wait for God. I hemmed and hawed about that, too, thinking, *I need to do something. No, I need to wait for God.* I wanted to meet a nice Christian man. I didn't want an Ishmael in my life."

Alyssa purchased a membership to an online Christian dating site. But after one day, she felt awkward about it and tried to cancel and get a refund. The site wouldn't let her cancel, and she was told she needed to keep the membership for three months whether she used it or not. The *very next day*, Wes found her online. He simply sent a smile emoji. She never connected with or dated any other man on the site and believes she had joined (and wasn't allowed to cancel) just long enough for Wes to find *her*.

"God's hand was all over our relationship" Alyssa said. They married just before she turned 33, and their daughter, Olivia, was born three years later.

"I wouldn't have met Wes if I hadn't been injured. I also wouldn't have volunteered for an organization I fell in love with [Dynamic Church Planting International], where I found my passion." God worked through Alyssa's disability to get her to the place where He could work *His* will in her life.

Looking back at God's track record of faithfulness—in helping her find her husband and her passion in life—has helped Alyssa look forward with faith to what God will continue to do. She has learned that she can trust Him with the unknown because she realizes He is the God of perfect timing.

"Now if I were to lose my job or my husband or little Olivia, I know nothing is mine. The home, the cars, *nothing* is truly mine." The perspective that everything she has is on loan from God changed the trajectory of Alyssa's life.

GLORIFYING GOD THROUGH IT ALL

Today, Alyssa is able to share in public corporate settings her history with mental illness and depression and where she is now as a board-certified behavioral analyst, working in a clinic that serves autistic children and adolescents.

"People are often shocked when they hear my story because they don't expect someone who lives an independent life to have struggled with mental illness," she said. "Many who have experienced what I've been through aren't able to grow through it.

"The theory is that everyone is predisposed to OCD. A traumatic event in life can switch it on," said Alyssa. Thus, doctors have told her the probability that her daughter will have mental illness is high. But Alyssa's assurance that her heavenly Father is in control of all things allows her to rest in His care and parent her daughter one day at a time to the best of her and Wes's ability. She chooses not to worry or obsess about what little Olivia may struggle with in the future. Her baby girl is God's too.

The key to Alyssa's health and freedom, she said, is not only being closely connected to Jesus, but being involved in support groups with other believers who experience unity because they are all indwelt by the Holy Spirit.

"If I were to go on alone, and not know that God is my solid rock to lean on, I can't imagine how lonely I would be," she said. "To not have the assurance that God is there would feel so hopeless." (For more of Alyssa's coping recommendations if you're struggling with

The Loneliness of Suffering and Loss

anxiety, depression, or mental illness, see "Struggling with Anxiety, Depression, or Mental Illness?" on page 243.)

WHY GOD ALLOWS SUFFERING

Perhaps you've asked at one time or another why God would allow you or someone you love to suffer. In their book *10 Essentials for New Christians*, Stan Jantz and Bruce Bickel explain it this way:

> God created a perfect world without sin and without suffering, but it was a world where choice existed...Because humanity chose to disobey God, sin entered the world, and with it suffering and evil...Because God is altogether holy, he is not capable of causing suffering, but he does allow it. While that may seem harsh, think of it this way. If God did not allow suffering and evil, he would have to destroy everything evil that causes suffering, including us! But out of his great love and mercy, God not only allows us to live, but he has given us a way to get back into a right relationship with him (Romans 5:6-11).[2]

Why does God allow suffering? Because if He were to eliminate it, He would have to destroy everything evil, including mankind. You and I sin, and that causes suffering to us and to others. Sinful people (and that's all of us, according to Romans 3:23) hurt others. Sinful people drive drunk and swerve into another lane and kill others. Sinful people make mistakes and do things they later regret. Sinful people think of themselves first and hurt others in relationships. Humans, another word for sinners, are capable of causing suffering through mistakes, negligence, ignorance, and selfishness. So, why does God allow suffering? Because God is gracious and has decided not to bring this present world to an end just yet. And God's desire is that our suffering will drive us to find Him as the answer and antidote to all suffering.

God's desire is that our suffering will drive us to find
Him as the answer and antidote to all suffering.

THE TREASURE IN OUR TRIALS

In the Old Testament, we read of Job, who suffered profusely. And his reward, mentioned at the end of the book, is evident in his proclamation, "I know that You can do all things, and that no purpose of Yours can be thwarted…I have heard of You by the hearing of the ear; but now my eye sees You" (42:2, 5 NASB 1995). Through his many difficulties and losses, Job gained a much more intimate relationship with God, Whom he didn't have the chance to know by reading the Scriptures we have today, or by experiencing the indwelling Holy Spirit of God. Job's suffering helped him experience God at a *personal* level, and he came out of it so much richer in every way.*

What did Alyssa gain as a result of her struggles?

"God has been the solid rock in my life," she said. "He has brought me strength in my weakest moments, comfort in my most trying times, and showed me so much grace and mercy when I did not deserve it.

"I have never questioned Him being there with me, but I have questioned why I was put through a trial. In hindsight, I see that His plan was far greater than anything I could have imagined. Now when I am struggling, I pray that God gives me the strength to get through it and to be thankful for the opportunity to grow closer to Him."

Through Alyssa's suffering with mental illness, a physical injury resulting in multiple surgeries, a delayed dream, disappointments, confusion, financial uncertainty, and loss, she

- gained a far closer relationship with God

---

* I encourage you to read the entire book of Job in one or two sittings. It's an eye-opening insight into the sovereignty of God and an easy, poetic read.

- discovered the value and support of gathering with other believers

- developed a deeper understanding of Scripture and God's purpose for her

- learned to trust God with every detail of her life

- saw Him as her Provider in every way

- developed the ability to listen for His still, small voice and follow His lead (like responding to Wes's smile emoji or taking a phone call from a friend she hadn't heard from in two years, who happened to direct her to a postpartum support group right when she needed it)

- realized that her purpose was to be *in* relationship with God, not necessarily *do* things for Him

Our character is shaped by our struggles. I have often thought of what my life would look like if I had everything I wanted, if I had never been hurt, if I was always comfortable and circumstances always went my way. Honestly? I'd be a selfish, entitled narcissist. Pain, disappointments, and unmet expectations in my life are what have drawn me closer to my Lord. My suffering has humbled me too. Misunderstandings in relationships have caused me to spend time seeking to know the mind and heart of God in the matter. The loneliest times in my life have drawn me closer to the One who has promised to never leave me nor forsake me. It's the struggles that have strengthened my walk with Jesus. And I imagine the same is true for you. Who would you be without the struggles that have shaped you?

Sometimes we tend to look to things like therapy, our culture, social media, comparison with others, personal affirmation, and so on to fill the gaping holes in our hearts and heal the wounds life has left us. But only when we go to the cross of Jesus, where He bore all our pain and suffering, can we begin to grow and experience healing. I love how one author stated it:

> Everything that God does is perfectly good and emanates out of His goodness—including His justice and discipline. We can be confident that in every way possible He is good to us, even when we cannot understand how it is so. He delights in blessing us, and His plans and will for us always have our ultimate good in mind.[3]

This author continues, "Every decision or life direction you and I face on this journey is shaped by how the cross shapes us. You may be weary, conflicted, confused, or unsure of your next steps, but in the shadow of the cross of our redemption, your path is sure and your true treasure is waiting."[4]

That is our prescription for power, our medication for meaningfulness, our secret to strength—the cross of Christ, which becomes our intersection from which we turn from our old way of doing things and start up His path of living by His power and victory. We see ourselves as He sees us. We make our decisions as He would make them. We trust Him first and foremost as we begin to trust others. And He shows us "life to the full," as He promised in John 10:10.

You and I suffer so God can make us more like His Son, Jesus. A verse we love to quote when we're going through struggles and hardships is Romans 8:28: "We know that God causes all things to work together for good to those who love God, to those who are called according to His purpose." But we need to get in the habit of quoting the first part of the next verse as well, which clarifies the "good" that God is working in all things: "Those whom He foreknew, He also predestined to become conformed to the image of His Son."

That is why you and I struggle, dear friend. And when you surrender your struggles to God, He promises to make you more like His perfect Son. Your difficulties are molding you into the image of Christ. That is the true treasure in your trials.

> Your difficulties are molding
> you into the image of Christ. That is
> the true treasure in your trials.

LOVED, NOT ABANDONED

God promises He will not leave us to suffer alone. Yet abandonment by someone you trusted (like a parent, or a spouse) can make you vulnerable to thoughts that God might abandon you too. I've often imagined that to be abandoned by someone you love would be bad enough. But to wonder whether you've been abandoned by God must be the loneliest feeling on earth. I am convinced today that because of God's great love for us, that will never happen.

More than 20 years ago, I learned a valuable lesson from Edie, a woman I looked up to as a spiritual mentor. She had been married longer and had been parenting longer than I had, she had been a pastor's wife twice as long, and she had dealt with many situations in life that I hadn't yet encountered. Besides her experience and maturity, Edie was gracious, authentic, so humble, and a true friend.

One day as we shared lunch, I asked Edie to tell me about a time in her life when she felt alone. I never forgot her answer: "When I was diagnosed with cancer for the first time, I had a difficult time believing God still loved me."

I was shocked to hear Edie say that. By that time, she had survived four bouts of cancer and was strong in her faith. Upon hearing of her reaction to her initial cancer diagnosis, I wondered how I would respond if I ever found myself in her shoes.

As Edie talked, I prayed silently: *Please Lord, if my time comes, don't let me think for a second that You don't love me anymore. I know that with Your help I could get through cancer. But I don't think I could get through a single day believing You no longer loved me.*

Edie shared with me the ways she experienced God's love for her, and she gave me some golden nuggets of wisdom. I eventually forgot about that conversation—until 20 years later, when my sister, rather unexpectedly, discovered a lump in my neck that the doctor was convinced was cancer.

Could it be, Lord? I prayed. I went to a doctor, took blood tests, and got an ultrasound the very next day. The ultrasound results were available to me online just a day later. The report showed a five-centimeter mass on my right thyroid lobe categorized as "high risk" because of "calcifications, uneven texture, and suspicious elements." That had me concerned. I did an internet search on thyroid cancer (something everyone tells you *not* to do) and felt much better after learning that 50 percent of adults have nodules on their thyroid lobes and 95 percent of them are benign.

Pretty good odds, I thought. So, I didn't worry about the lump anymore. Until the day of my biopsy, three weeks later.

After my endocrinologist pulled up the ultrasound image on her computer monitor, she said to me and my husband, "I want to know what this ugly thing is and what it's doing there." I felt sick to my stomach after seeing the grotesque blob that was not only inside of me but clinging abnormally to one of my body parts.

My doctor talked about possible diagnoses and courses of action, but all I heard were the words, "This does not look benign." In addition to a fine-needle biopsy of the mass, she also took ten tissue samples from several areas of the mass so she could run molecular scans of them against every known mutation of thyroid cancer. "If this biopsy comes back benign, but atypical, I'm not going to be satisfied with that," she said. "So I'm preparing now for more conclusive tests."

For three weeks, as I awaited that appointment to take the biopsy, and then for another four weeks as I awaited the results of the molecular scans, I had never felt so loved. Every incident from the moment the mass was discovered pointed to God's sovereignty and perfect timing. He showed such grace in allowing me to get appointments quickly and receive encouraging words from friends and family who were praying. I even believed if the lump were malignant that God was surely singling me out with the privilege of enduring this for His glory.

As I look back now, I realize my thinking was not typical for someone who may have had an aggressive form of thyroid cancer. Humanly speaking, I should have been scared out of my mind! I could have easily found myself questioning God's love, not feeling overwhelmed by it. It was then that I remembered that silent prayer from 20 years earlier: *Please Lord, if my time comes, don't let me think for a second that You don't love me anymore.*

For two decades, I believed my greatest fear was getting cancer. But God knew, and remembered, that my greatest fear was not a diagnosis, but the feeling that I was no longer loved by Him. God's tender response to me during that uncertainty gave me the confidence that, whatever this lump was, it would not result in devastation because He had already shown me that I will never lose what matters to me most: His love, His comfort, His provision, His presence.

In His presence is fullness of joy, says Psalm 16:11. And I was experiencing it.

My biopsy results showed the mass was benign but atypical and my tissues were already undergoing further studies for the possibility of a cancerous mutation. Those results would give my doctor more information in terms of calculating my risks. In the meantime, I knew I was loved. And that was enough.

WHEN GOD DOESN'T DO WHAT WE ASK

My mysterious mass was downgraded to low risk once molecular scans came back showing no known mutation for thyroid cancer. My doctor gave me the option of monitoring it every four to six months via ultrasound, or having it surgically removed, which carried with it a risk that I could lose my voice permanently or experience a change in my vocal range. At that time, I had several upcoming speaking engagements, with plans for more, so losing my voice was not a risk I was willing to take. I felt complete peace about declining the surgery and giving God a chance to eliminate the tumor Himself. Besides, I was feeling loved and cared for, not just because of an initial benign report, but because God was distracting me from the uncertainties by confirming the absolute certainty of His love.

My first ultrasound to monitor the mass, just three months later, showed God had not eliminated it. He didn't even shrink it. Instead, He allowed it to grow in all directions! My heart sank. I knew I was following His lead to wait upon Him instead of rushing into surgery. But why didn't God do what I had faith He would do during that time of waiting?

In that long hour or two of complete discouragement, I heard His still, small voice in my heart: *I know you don't understand. But now you know what it's like to trust Me even when I don't do what you ask.*

What *love*. Here I was, writing a book to encourage those who are lonely that God is still there even when He doesn't appear to be giving us what we asked for. And I realized God would rather have me write from a genuine heart of experience than from an ivory tower of theory. He is still good, even when He doesn't answer our prayers the way we had hoped.

My doctor took my ultrasound images to a room full of endocrinologists and head and neck surgeons to get their consensus on a benign mass that wasn't acting benign. They recommended that I should have the mass removed immediately as it might be an unknown mutation for an aggressive form of cancer. It took an additional two months to get on the surgeon's calendar, and by then, the "immediate surgery" was still another 30 days out.

Upon realizing I was waiting a total of three months while this mass continued to grow, God seemed to whisper, once again, to my heart: *I will keep you here a bit longer because during this time of uncertainty, you and I have never been closer.*

GOD'S GOT THIS

When things don't go your way, remember how much God loves you. When prayers aren't answered as you had hoped, and when He keeps you in a holding pattern where you are dependent upon Him for the air in your lungs, the health in your body, and the ability to get out of bed each morning, remember He still has a plan—and it might be more about you and Him than about what you're praying for.

Because we live in a world where we get instant search results on the internet or our phones, instant pain relief from certain medications, instant heated food from our microwaves, and instant access to a myriad of streaming services all with the click of a button, we certainly find it more difficult to wait upon God for His timing, which today can feel slower than ever. Yet God's ways and His timing continue to be perfect (Psalm 18:30). Even when the world seems to be racing by us, God is still at work, steadily and perfectly bringing about His best for our lives.

Are you willing to stay in whatever season of uncertainty you are in right now if it keeps you closer to God's heart than ever? Are you willing to go through more dark or uncertain times if it reveals to you more of His presence, His provision, and His protection? And if it means He is doing a work in you that will help you minister to others in more compassionate ways? I've learned by now that God will never take anything from you without giving you somethinng better.

That is how much God loves *you* too. Trust Him, my friend. When it seems He's far off or not doing anything, know without a doubt He has you right where He wants you—up next to His heart.

You are not alone in your suffering or loss. You are being empowered by the One who is molding and shaping you into a closer representation of His Son.

BEING INTENTIONAL

1. In the space below, write out your biggest fear during this season of your life. (God already knows what it is, but this is your way of getting it onto paper and setting it before Him.)

2. Now write a short prayer in the space below, surrendering this fear to Jesus, who knows you inside and out and has every ability to calm your heart.

3. Have you ever wondered who you would be today without the struggles that have shaped you? What has God allowed in your life that has shaped you into the person you are now?

4. Read the following verses and record what each says about what God is capable of, or what He promises:

   Exodus 14:14:

   Psalm 71:20-21:

Psalm 139:1-3:

Isaiah 55:8-11:

Matthew 11:28-30:

Romans 8:28-29:

2 Corinthians 1:3-4:

Hebrews 13:5:

5. How do you think increased use of your digital devices might diminish your time getting to know God and trusting Him?

How might your time or dependence upon digital devices prevent you from seeking out a mentor or someone to disciple you during the difficult seasons of your life?

A CHALLENGE TO HELP YOU GROW

Write out a prayer below, asking God to bring a trusted Christian friend into your life (or open your eyes to see who is already in your life) whom you can talk with about your struggles.

PART 2

RECONNECTING WITH YOUR HEART

Now that we've learned about reconnecting with God and we understand that He's with us, He's for us, and He has a purpose for whatever we face, we can start gaining the confidence to live in healthy relationships with others so we don't feel so lonely.

This section will help you learn more about your heart, what might be keeping you from forming friendships or trusting others, and how you can slow down and become more intentional about fostering friendships. As you trust God more, you'll grow in your trust of others and give of yourself as Jesus gave Himself for you.

CHAPTER 4

THE LONELINESS OF INADEQUACY AND COMPARISON

Developing a Servant Mindset

The less you are in your own eyes, the more fit you are for the Lord Jesus, and the more welcome will you be at the throne of grace.[1]

JAMES SMITH

Rachel never felt more inadequate than after she graduated from college and started working for a Christian organization in a third-world country. She was beyond excited to get to the Horn of Africa and felt God had called her and equipped her for the task. But everything was so different.

"I had no friends and no family with me, I spoke zero words of the local language, and I felt like a stranger in every way," Rachel said. "I am five-feet-ten with sandy blonde hair and green eyes; I stood out like a very tall and pale sore thumb in my African village. From cooking, to shopping in the open-air market, to laundry, to drinking water, to showering, every little thing was different and had to be relearned."

God provided Rachel with an American roommate, Candace, who had arrived on the field nine months before her.

"Candace was such a blessing and took care of me well, but in those first couple of months, I remember feeling so helpless and so lonely," Rachel said. "It was a time in my life when I was deeply uncomfortable, but it was a blessing that led to intimacy and a reliance on Christ. In my struggle of being uncomfortable, I learned to trust and depend on God. Daily I would run to the Lord feeling completely insufficient, and daily, He would speak to me from His Word and show me His sufficiency."

After being in the village for months, Rachel developed the ability to communicate and to start to understand what was happening around her. She and her teammates became closer, and she had more local friends.

"But life still felt so hard," Rachel said. "I looked at my roommate, who seemed to pick up language and culture so quickly and who seemed so comfortable. Everyone said that she was 'made for the Horn of Africa.' She was a naturally good cook, an expert linguist, her social battery never ran empty. She had a vibrant and committed prayer life, she wasn't distracted by boys, she didn't like watching Netflix or wasting her time other ways, and I barely ever saw her sit down. She didn't seem to struggle at all. It seemed like she was better at everything than I was.

"As I watched her, I began to feel little twinges of jealousy. I would hear whispers from the devil: *Candace is better than you. You are useless. Why do you even bother living here?* I began to feel like I was failing, and to believe the lie that if I was uncomfortable, I didn't belong there. However, God reminded me through His Word that my job wasn't to be successful in everything I did, and I didn't need to be or act exactly like Candace. The greatest commandment is to love the Lord your God with all your heart, mind, and strength. If I could love God with everything I had, that was enough."

Rachel said that as she and her roommate grew closer, "There were still twinges of jealousy I had to actively fight against. But I also began to see God's character displayed so beautifully through her and through our relationship. We couldn't be more different, but God brought us together to accomplish His purposes. Candace came from a broken home where she had never been able to be comfortable and God gave her the gift of feeling comfortable in Africa—for His glory. And I came from a great home where I never had to be uncomfortable, and God gave me the gift of feeling uncomfortable in Africa so that I might rely on Him—for His glory."

Rachel was able to see the beauty in her and Candace's differences. But natural feelings of inadequacy, comparison, and competition could've easily divided them and prevented them from accomplishing what they did in Africa while serving God together.

OUR SENSE OF INADEQUACY

We all feel inadequate at one time or another. Usually this happens when we forget Who we should be comparing ourselves to. Our constant need to compete with and compare ourselves to other women is another piece of shrapnel lodged into our old nature. Competing and comparing can not only harm our relationships with others, it can make us feel especially lonely and unable to live God's purposes for us. Because of the prevalence of social media, competing and comparing is easier than ever before. We just scroll and compare. We see and become jealous. We constantly observe others' achievements and can sink another level lower in our sense of inadequacy and our pit of loneliness.

Macey, a young wife and mom of three, told me, "I feel inadequate or unworthy because I'm not living up to the standards that have been set for me, like being perfect."

But whose standards are we trying to live up to? The standards and expectations of others? Or of Jesus?

And where did we get the idea that we must be perfect?
Oh, that's right: Jesus said it.

OUR CALL TO PERFECTION

In His Sermon on the Mount, Jesus said, "You shall be perfect, as your heavenly Father is perfect" (Matthew 5:48 NASB 1995). Of course, perfection isn't possible this side of heaven and Jesus knew that. He was sharing kingdom principles with the crowd and telling them their character and behavior toward one another should go beyond the average person's. Those who wanted to follow Jesus and live for the kingdom of God were to strive to be perfect in *character*, *behavior*, and *generous living* toward one another.

Here is the context in which Jesus commanded perfection from His followers and all who came to hear Him preach:

> You have heard that it was said, "You shall love your neighbor and hate your enemy." But I say to you, love your enemies and pray for those who persecute you, so that you may prove yourselves to be sons of your Father who is in heaven; for He causes His sun to rise on the evil and the good, and sends rain on the righteous and the unrighteous. For if you love those who love you, what reward do you have? Even the tax collectors, do they not do the same? And if you greet only your brothers and sisters, what more are you doing than others? Even the Gentiles, do they not do the same? Therefore you shall be perfect, as your heavenly Father is perfect (Matthew 5:43-48).

Did you catch that? Jesus wanted us to be perfect in our *love* for one another. He wanted us to shoot for perfection when it came to how well we treated someone. If there was competition involved, it was that we be better at loving someone than they were at loving us.

And yet when you and I desire perfection, is it our *character* and *love for others* that we're focused on? Or is it our appearance, abilities, and achievements? From what I've observed in my own life and in the lives of countless women I've ministered to over the years, our tendency is to want to be perfect in all we *do* for our own sense of value, and for the approval of other women who are looking on.

Friend, shortly after Jesus told us to be perfect, He died for the sins of the world so that—through our faith in Him and His righteousness imputed to us—we could be seen as perfect by our Father in heaven. He did what was necessary so that we could be perfect in God's eyes. Yet so often we feel inadequate for not being perfect in our own power and in the ways we wish we were. We also tend to feel we're not making the mark when it comes to doing enough for God, our families, and those we love. And we often struggle with the loneliness of feeling we're not measuring up to our own standards of perfection.

THE "PRESSURES" WE FACE

Kadee, a military wife whom you met on page 12, recently received her master's degree in social work. She got that degree while raising five young children. Yet she feels weighed down by the pressure of perfectionism almost daily.

"Personally, the pressure from the world on women to be a certain way or to be able to achieve makes me feel inadequate," Kadee said. She's not the only one who feels that way. Nearly every woman I interviewed for this book, regardless of her age, felt pressure to be perfect, to succeed, to strive for more than what she had. And they felt lacking in comparison to others.

Where do we get this idea that the world is putting pressure on us?

- From magazine, internet, and social media photos portraying the perfect face or body we feel we'll never have?

- From Pinterest and Instagram shots showing DIY projects we believe we could never accomplish?

- From brag reports (aka social media posts) of all one accomplishes or experiences on what looks like a perfect day in their perfect life when that post represents just a fraction of their experience, not the whole story?

- From the words others say that sound condemning, even though we know from God's Word that our value rests in Him?

While we know God is with us and for us, and has a purpose for everything we struggle with, hurtful questions or comments from others can still cause us to feel we are lacking in some way. And that can make us lonely.

Kadee added, "Being in God's Word every day has helped me draw near to Him when I'm feeling pressure from the world or my circumstances."

OUR MEASURING STICK

Young women have told me they often compare themselves to others around their same age and stage of life and feel they haven't done much. Accomplished single women, regardless of their age, have told me they often compare themselves to married women with careers and families and feel they are lacking. It's easy for us to look around at others and feel we're missing the boat—or at least a better life. You and I can always find someone doing more or better than us and sink into feelings of inadequacy by comparison.

Tiffany, a young married professional, said, "Maybe it's just the type A perfectionist in me, but I struggle with feeling inadequate or unworthy when I feel as though I don't perform up to standard—whether that's at work, in social situations, as a wife, maintaining friendships, and so on. I often listen to my harsh inner critic rather than who Christ says that I am."

LISTENING TO A NEW SONG

Do you have a harsh inner critic as well? That internal voice specializes in pointing out what is wrong with you and why you aren't as good or proficient as the other woman in your office, church, or neighborhood. I know you've heard that inner critic—whether it's your own voice, the voice of someone in your past, or the voice of the enemy of your soul (the one who whispers accusations at you, wanting you to feel shame).

You and I must train our ears to listen for the voice of truth and clear direction. I refer to this as tuning our ears to the Holy Spirit's frequency. We can do that when we know what His voice "sounds" like. And the best way to recognize His "spoken voice" is to know His written Word.

In John 10:27, Jesus said, "My sheep listen to My voice, and I know them, and they follow Me."

While I've never heard God's voice *audibly*, I have often heard His voice through the wisdom of mature believers. I've sensed His direction and presence through divinely arranged circumstances in my life. And I've heard His voice through His trustworthy Word that sometimes echoes in my ears through what I call His whispers on my heart—those thoughts, based on His Word, that come sometimes at random, with a conviction, warning, encouragement, or affirmation. I've learned to trust such whispers of guidance when I'm certain they don't contradict God's Word or defy His character in any way.*

I'm so encouraged by the story in 1 Kings 19 that tells us what God's voice is like. When the prophet Elijah was worn out from

---

* If you struggle with hearing God's voice, I've written a detailed chapter on that topic in my book *Letting God Meet Your Emotional Needs* (Eugene, OR: Harvest House, 2000).

ministry and feeling inadequate for what lay ahead of him, God saw his discouragement and told him to go out on the face of a rock so he could hear God's voice. And get this! God's voice wasn't in a tornado-like wind that tore the mountains apart and shattered the rocks. His voice wasn't in an earthquake that followed the wind, nor in a blazing fire that followed the earthquake. Rather, God's voice was in a "gentle blowing" — a soft breeze, a loving whisper (verses 11-13).

That story reminds me that God's voice is not a booming thunder of demands or expectations. It's not a howling wind urging us to outperform our girlfriends or win the "Most Capable Woman" award through more strain and stress. His is not the loud voice from a coach on the sidelines ready to revel in our victory or be humiliated by our defeat. His is the voice of a Good Shepherd whose sheep (and sheep tend to be timid) know His voice and trust His lead (John 10:11-17). Oswald Chambers said, "As we listen, our ears become sensitive, and like Jesus, we will hear God all the time."[2]

Oh, how I want to hear more of that gentle voice of loving affirmation and godly direction, don't you? We start tuning our ears to the Holy Spirit's gentle whispers on our hearts by deleting the old playlist that Satan has been warping our minds with for far too long, and plugging in to a new set of tunes…the ones from His Word that tell us how very much we mean to Him.

YOUR SOURCE OF SIGNIFICANCE

You and I are tremendously significant because we are made in the image of God, stamped with His likeness. We are like Him in our abilities to reason, to be creative, and to manage. We are like our Maker in that we are able to exhibit His character as we yield to the control of His Holy Spirit.

Are you significant? Very much so. But are you adequate? Not on your own. None of us are. Jesus alone is our adequacy — and our ticket to tremendous. We depend on Him for our strength, our wisdom, and even our righteousness (which was imputed to us when we accepted, by faith, His atoning death for us on the cross). Here is what Scripture says about your adequacy in Christ, regardless of how you might feel on any given day or when comparing yourself to anyone else.

1. You are "awesomely and wonderfully made."

In Psalm 139:13-16, we are given a description of the care God took when He wove us together and saw our physical development in our mothers' wombs. No other passage of Scripture goes into such detail about our creation and our significance to our Creator and heavenly Father's heart. The Hebrew word for "fearfully" or "awesomely" (*yārē'*) speaks of the sacred and reverent aspect of how God made us, and the Hebrew word translated "wonderfully" (*pālâ*) emphasizes God's craftsmanship and speaks to how we are distinct from all the rest of God's creation. We alone bear God's image—no other creature does. Each one of us is a magnificent work of God's craftsmanship, which speaks of His design for us (Ephesians 2:10). This doesn't put us onto any kind of standard of perfection. We cannot be compared to anything or to anyone else because we are uniquely and specially designed by God for His own design and purpose. God has made us what we are, and when we let Him, He is able to accomplish His purposes in us.

In His perfect plan, God made you exactly the way He wanted in order to accomplish His purposes through you. Let that give you an incredible shot of self-worth!

2. You have been adopted by God and given the privilege to call Him Daddy.

Romans 8:15 tells us God has given us the spirit of adoption, whereby we can call Him "Daddy"—the most affectionate term we could use for a loving, doting father. Why were we adopted? Because we are all God's *creation*, but we are not all God's *children*. He had to adopt us out of the clutches of Satan, the "father of lies" (John 8:44), through our faith in His Son Jesus, so we could be redeemed of our sin and become a child of His. Think about that. He sought us out and went through the grueling, bloody death-of-His-Son adoption process to make us His own.

3. You are heir of all that He has.

As His adopted child, you are also an heiress of all that He has, and Ephesians 1 tells us it's yours *now*, not just one day in heaven. As a joint heir of the kingdom of God, you are considered His royal daughter with complete access to Him and all that He owns. (Please pause and let that sink in for a moment or two before moving on. You may even want to read the first chapter of Ephesians now as a refresher course in all that is yours. It's pretty amazing!)

4. You possess His authority while here on earth.

Jesus told His followers in John 14:13-14 that through their faith in Him, whatever they asked for in His name, He would do. That privilege is ours, too, through the authority we have in our relational standing with Him. There really is power in your prayers when you pray for what Jesus would pray for because of Who you know and Who loves you.

In addition to those benefits of knowing God, Ephesians 3:20 tells us God is "able to do far more abundantly beyond all that we ask or think, according to the power that works within us."

Whaaattt? That's incredible. You and I, by knowing God and relying on His power through us, are not only significant and super-adequate, we have *superpowers*—super, God-enabled power to live incredible, unstoppable lives all because of Who loves us and what He's given us.

And yet we still compare ourselves to our girlfriends and feel we come up short? Could it be that we are spending so much time with our digital devices observing the highlight reels of others, reading public opinion, and taking in what this culture is proclaiming, that we are losing a sense of what God thinks of us? Perhaps we've become so attuned to this culture's voice and opinions that we've forgotten God's—especially when it comes to who we are in His eyes.

WHY WE COMPARE

We may not measure our self-worth or success against others consciously, but we tend to do it constantly. We try to compensate either by being critical and judgmental of others, or we shrink into deeper feelings of inadequacy because we think we fall short.

Timothy Keller wrote this in his book *The Freedom of Self-Forgetfulness*: "The way the normal human ego tries to fill its emptiness and deal with its discomfort is by comparing itself to other people. All the time."[3] "We say we are proud of our accomplishments," Keller continued, "but only when measured in light of everyone else's."

Keller added, "We are only proud of being *more* successful, *more* intelligent, or *more* good-looking than the next person."[4] Pride, he summarized, is the pleasure of having more than the next person.[5] (Are you feeling a tinge of conviction here? Trust me, I feel it too.)

Dear friend, whose expectations are you hoping to meet when it comes to your sense of adequacy? Who is your measuring stick when it comes to excellence or self-affirmation? A social media influencer? A celebrity? That friend from high school with whom you've always competed but with whom you've always come up short? An older or younger sister? Your ex's new girlfriend or wife?

Whom do you want to outdo? And whom do you set as the ideal standard for imitation?

BE THE BEST VERSION OF...WHO?

Instead of striving to be more like Christ, we often strive to be like someone else, or simply to be *more*—more accomplished, more confident, or more of what we believe is genuinely and uniquely *us*. It's common to now say or hear the phrase, "Be the best version of yourself." And yet that's a recipe for disaster. Self-improvement projects are temporary at best. Disastrous at worst. There's only One who can improve—or rather transform—us, and that is Jesus.

Instead of striving to be a better version of you, strive to imitate *Jesus*. That was the apostle Paul's goal. He had a prideful past and felt very accomplished and spiritually successful as one of Israel's religious elite. Yet upon meeting Jesus, he considered all his accomplishments and bragging points as "mere rubbish" (Philippians 3:8)—as worthless as dog dung (MSG)—compared to the surpassing value of knowing Christ. Paul proclaimed that his accomplishments and adequacy in himself didn't mean squat compared to the riches of who he was and all he had in his newfound relationship with the resurrected Jesus. Thus, instead of more of himself, he wanted more of Jesus.

God has made it so very clear in His Word that once we are redeemed through the death and resurrection of His Son, He has made us significant. He sees us not as merely adequate, which means "good enough." He sees us as stupendous. He sees us as He sees His own perfect Son.

God has made it so very clear in His Word that once we are redeemed through the death and resurrection of His Son, He has made us significant.

NEVER ENOUGH, BUT THAT'S OKAY

That feeling that you are not enough is a great place to start in your journey toward discovering the "immeasurably more" that God can do through you.*

In today's society, it is popular to say and believe, "I am enough." We're told that through self-confidence and self-love we can achieve anything. But you and I are *not* enough. Only Jesus is. Jesus working through you is *more* than enough. If we try to reach the enough stage without Him, our pursuit will always end in disappointment.

What if God's grace and enabling (rather than your lack) were foremost in your mind every time you saw another woman doing, looking, or behaving better than you? Instead of thinking, *Why can't I be as exceptional as her?*, your worth in Christ could be bolstered by these thoughts:

> *Except for God's grace, I would be able to do nothing at all.*
>
> *By God's grace, I can do what He has purposed me to do.*
>
> *It is God's grace that leads me; therefore, He's the One I do all things for.*

What if you were to adopt one of those proclamations and say it aloud every time you started to feel inadequate? I guarantee it would change the trajectory of your thoughts and actions. Look at those three phrases again. Do you see the common element in each of those statements? It's *God.* More of Him and less of you and me. Oswald Chambers said, "The well of your incompleteness runs deep, but make the effort to look away from yourself and to look toward Him."[6]

---

* Ephesians 3:20 tells us God is able to do "immeasurably more than all we ask or imagine, according to his power that is at work within us" (NIV).

THE BOTTOM LINE, AND IT'S NOT US

As I sat down to write this chapter, I originally subtitled it "Seeing Yourself as God Does." Then I considered changing the subtitle to "Finding Your Affirmation in Him." After all, the solution to our feelings of inadequacy and our tendency to compare is to see ourselves as beautifully and wonderfully made as God sees us, and to find our personal affirmation in who we are to Him.

So much has been written about our need to see ourselves as God sees us and find our affirmation in Him, yet we keep playing the comparison game and nurturing our feelings of inadequacy in spite of what we've been told from Scripture.

The solution to our feelings of inadequacy and our tendency to compare is to see ourselves as beautifully and wonderfully made as God sees us, and to find our personal affirmation in who we are to Him.

I'm convinced we can hear about and memorize our identity statements in Scripture and keep reading about how much we're loved, how much we're blessed in being made in the image of God, and how much we are bursting with potential because of His power within us, and yet *still* struggle with comparison, perfectionism, and a focus that is all about us and our inadequacies. That's because we still live in our fallen human bodies and we are prone to thinking about ourselves, our weaknesses and our failures and wounds.

As I mentioned earlier, you are *not* enough. Neither am I. We never will be. That's why we need a Savior. *He is enough*. And He always will be. Furthermore, His Spirit dwells within us, giving us the ability to live as He calls us to live. Now, how can that truth amount to a different way of thinking, living, and serving others rather than ourselves? When we do what the subtitle of this chapter tells us to do: Develop a servant mindset. You and I have a master, Jesus Christ, Who has also made us His children and fellow heirs with Him (Ephesians 1:4-6). Therefore, we have an obligation and privilege to serve Him and others...and it's the ultimate medicine for the disease of self and a cure for the ailment of loneliness.

You and I often feel inadequate because something brushes up against our ego. Because someone hurts us and we cave inward. Because our self-esteem balloon was burst as we got a look at how damaged we really are. That's reality, my precious sister in Christ. So, let's renew our minds and start thinking differently when it comes to other women so we can stop thinking so much about ourselves.

RENEW YOUR MIND

Romans 12:2 tells us not to be conformed to the world and its way of thinking, but to be transformed into the new you—the one like Jesus. How? The rest of the verse tells us: by the renewing of your mind.

You can renew your mind when you follow these steps.

1. Correct your thought patterns.

Capture those incorrect thoughts from your old, unredeemed mind, or from this world, and correct them with the truths of God's Word, which are meant to point you toward new ways of thinking. Perhaps you've had these kinds of thoughts:

- *I know God created me and He doesn't make mistakes, but I wish He had made me differently.*

- *I wish I could be as talented as she is.*

- *I am not as useful to God as she is; therefore, I'm not as loved or favored.*

Often, it's our insecurities, our feelings of inadequacy, and our wounds from the past that make us think these ways. But when we are aware of our negative thoughts (and anything that raises itself up against the knowledge of God—2 Corinthians 10:5), we can stop those thoughts in their tracks and correct them so they can't continue to infect us. Negative thoughts also make us feel we aren't friend-worthy or God-worthy. If we don't fully believe we're accepted by Christ, we will have a much harder time fully believing anyone else will accept us either.

When you have it settled in your heart what God thinks of you, your expectations of others and your willingness to do anything to please them will be replaced by an emotional stability and confidence in who you are in Christ and an ability to love others as *they* are, rather than seek their love for who *you* are.

2. Remember the true Source of significance.

The secret to significance is knowing its Source. And the source of significance is not ourselves. It's not our accomplishments, abilities, nor achievements. It's not our relationships. It's our Creator, Sustainer, and Enabler, God Himself. Everything is insignificant apart from Him. But when we are in relationship with Him, suddenly we are soaked with significance because of Who He is and why He has us here. Significance doesn't get any stronger or more solid than that!

3. Focus on facts, not feelings.

Feelings of insignificance are just that—feelings, not facts. And while we live in a day and age when we are encouraged to pay attention to our feelings—to embrace, obey, excuse, and express our feelings—we would do better to consider them a by-product that, at times, may not be real or accurate. You may have heard the saying, "Your feelings aren't right or wrong; they just are." It is more biblical to say, "Your feelings aren't necessarily based on truth, but the facts are."

You may be feeling that you are inadequate, unworthy, insignificant. This might be based on past wounds, current circumstances, or your fears about the future. But your feelings constantly change, depending on your mood or circumstances. In contrast, the facts about who you are, which are recorded in God's Word, don't change. They stand the test of time.

In her devotional *Streams in the Desert*, Mrs. Charles E. Cowman wrote:

> God never wants us to look at our feelings. Self may want us to; and Satan may want us to. But God wants us to face facts, not feelings; the facts of Christ and of His finished and perfect work [for] us.
>
> When we face these precious facts, and believe them because God says they are facts, God will take care of our feelings.
>
> God never gives feeling to enable us to trust Him; God never gives feeling to encourage us to trust Him; God never gives feeling to show that we have already and utterly trusted Him.
>
> God gives feeling only when He sees that we trust Him apart from all feeling, resting on His own Word, and on His own faithfulness to His promise.
>
> Never until then can the feeling (which is from God) possibly come; and God will give the feeling in such a measure and at such a time as His love sees best for the individual case.
>
> We must choose between facing toward our feelings and facing toward God's facts. Our feelings may be as uncertain as the sea or the shifting sands. God's facts are as certain as

the Rock of Ages, even Christ Himself, who is the same yesterday, today, and forever.[7]

A GAME-CHANGER

In Genesis 2:18, we learn that women were created to be helpers. It is part of our DNA to want to help or support someone, encourage them, and be a part of their team. However, we've turned that around and often feel we will fulfill our purpose once we are *with* someone, *supported by* someone—loved, cherished, and desired *by* someone else. But when we realize we are valued, supported, encouraged, cherished, and desired by the Living God, that's a game-changer.

Remember, God has said, "I have loved you with an everlasting love" (Jeremiah 31:3). He has said He will never leave us nor forsake us (Hebrews 13:5). These truths are meant to help steady us and will spur us to keep seeking Him and trusting Him. And we are able to encourage and affirm others and be a better friend to them when we stop needing others to constantly encourage and affirm us. In God, we are no longer fragmented and lacking; we can find completion and not waste time on comparison, competition, or overcompensating.

The next time you're tempted to start measuring your inadequacies or comparing yourself to another woman, reverse the thought process. Instead of thinking about where you fall short, start thinking of someone who might feel the same way and focus on how you can encourage her. Be one who builds into others rather than one who seeks to boost herself. As you humble yourself and seek to lift up others, Christ will in turn lift you up (James 4:10).

BEING INTENTIONAL

1. In the space below, list three things about yourself that you are thankful for.

2. Now list three things you have had the privilege of experiencing that you know others would want to experience.

3. Read the following verses. Who should receive the credit and gratitude for all you have and everything you've experienced?

   Psalm 84:11:

   Matthew 7:11:

   James 1:17:

4. Which of the four descriptions of you on pages 99-100 will you focus on this week? How?

5. Why might friendships be difficult to sustain if you compete with or compare yourself to others?

6. What are some ways you can congratulate others rather than compete with or compare yourself to them?

7. Is there a source of secular, negative, or worldly thinking that you can trim from your daily routine so that you can tune your ears to hear more of God's truth than the world's voice? If so, indicate what it is and how you can avoid it.

   How can you make the truths from God's Word a greater part of your "daily intake"?

A CHALLENGE TO HELP YOU GROW

Pray today that God would bring someone to your mind who has experienced defeat recently. (They're all around us, we just need to ask God to open our eyes to notice them and their circumstances.) Then take the initiative to encourage that person through a phone call, a handwritten note sent through the mail, or an invitation to lunch.

CHAPTER 5

THE LONELINESS
OF BUSYNESS

Gifting Yourself Space for God and Friends

Both sin and busyness have the exact same
effect—they cut off your connection to God,
to other people, and even to your own soul.[1]

JOHN MARK COMER

I was surprised the day my daughter told me, "Mom, you don't have any friends. I'm not talking about writing clients or people you work with in ministry. You don't go out and spend time with girlfriends anymore."

I started to explain to Dana that of course I have friends. But in many ways, she was right. I had become so comfortable with working from home, connecting with writing clients via Zoom, and keeping in touch with friends on social media that I hadn't prioritized friendship time the way I had before the pandemic. I wasn't getting together with girlfriends anymore or meeting up with my mentors for lunch, or even networking in-person with author friends. I truly was spending a lot of time alone.

Dana opened my eyes to the fact that I wasn't being intentional about in-person relationships. And in the season of life I was in, and as busy as I was, I found it easy to justify my lack of friendship time on the basis that I was good with Jesus and didn't need more beyond that. I had adapted to the mindset, *Some things you have to give up if you want to excel at work and ministry.*

Wow, was I blinded. Now, as I near the sixth decade of my life, I have to constantly check myself to ensure I'm making enough time not only for God, but friendships too, because you and I can't get through life and grow spiritually in isolation. We were meant to have each other.

Did you notice I said *making* enough time, rather than *taking* enough time, or even *finding* enough time? We all *make* time for what is most important to us. If we wait until we can *find* time for what we want and need to do, the opportunities likely won't materialize. You and I must be intentional about cultivating friendships and spending physical time (not just virtual time behind a screen) with friends, or we will find ourselves facing loneliness more frequently.

What is the real reason you and I don't spend more time with friends? I think any of us would say we would *like* to spend more time with others, but we're too busy with the urgent, essential, day-to-day busyness that consumes our lives. Our ever-increasing to-do list, and the obligation to produce, accomplish, or simply keep our heads above water in our whirlwind schedules precludes us from the luxury of spending time with friends. We might even feel guilty if we spend time with a girlfriend or two because a husband, child, or aging parent may be complaining about wanting more time with us as it is. Or maybe we feel it's just too difficult to try to make friends these days. But cultivating friendships and deepening relationships with those we *need* in our lives is not a luxury. It's a necessity. Thinking you can go through life and its inevitable struggles without close friends to hold you steady is like thinking you can go into battle without armor.

YOUR NEED FOR ARMOR BEARERS

Years ago, my friend Barbara started referring to herself as my "armor bearer." She came up with that term right after my first book was released 25 years ago, because she's a woman who prays. She often prays for me—when I go out and speak, when I'm writing another book, when we connect over lunch at Chick-fil-A and she wants to know how she can help hold me up. She defends me, encourages me, builds into me. I'm never the same after I leave her presence. I'm always stronger and able to re-enter the spiritual battle we live in daily. I love her description of being my armor bearer—she bears me up in prayer and helps me carry what is too heavy for me to carry alone. I am so grateful to have had Barbara as my armor bearer for the past two decades of my life and counting. She is a friend worth making time for.

Connie is another one of my armor bearers. I met Connie after she read a couple of my books on marriage and contacted me about purchasing several more copies for her friends. Through the years, we've kept in touch and Connie has become a close friend and prayer partner. She often messages me at the perfect time, reminding me that even though she is 400 miles away, she is as close as a phone call or text message. Today, she and I are more like sisters. I love it when the Holy Spirit nudges her heart to reach out with an encouraging word or ask how she can pray for me. It makes me feel loved by both Connie and Jesus.

You need an armor bearer too. Someone to build you up, encourage you, and help you carry in prayer what you can't carry alone. And to find that person and maintain their presence and help in your life, you can't be too busy for friends.

THE TOLL OF BUSYNESS

Busyness not only produces stress and hinders us from pursuing friendships, it takes a toll on our perspective—and our level of loneliness—if we aren't careful to carve out time and space for God, ourselves, and our relationships. When we believe we can be more efficient and productive by staying in front of a screen, it further hinders us from getting out and being around others. After a while, we find ourselves overloaded with work and short on time to be with the people we love, and feeling as though we must do more.

We often measure our success by how busy we are or how productive we are in ministry or in "making progress for the kingdom." But God's kingdom consists of soul work that happens as people connect more deeply with Him first, and then with one another. Can we really say ministry is productive if it isn't impacting people?

As I began writing this book, I surveyed women ages 25-45 in particular and asked them what has served as their lifeline during times of loneliness (or what God has used to draw them closer to Himself in such times). Their answers (along with the answers from women ages 46-79) most often included one or more of the following activities:

1. Spending time with God in His Word

2. Spending time listening to worship music and praising Him (especially while out in nature)

3. Spending time with other like-minded women and opening up about their struggles

Notice how all three activities call for "spending time" with someone else. Obviously, we must invest time in our relationships with God and others, and these investments will help diminish our feelings of loneliness. In each of those time-spending priorities, there is someone other than us in the picture—we're either *sharing* our time with God or a like-minded friend, or both. Yet we have to set aside our digital devices now and then to truly make the time to spend with others. If we're honest with ourselves, we'll admit our devices have eaten into the time we could be spending with God in prayer and in His Word, and in building relationships with others.

THE LONELINESS OF BUSYNESS

A mom of two teenagers who often feels overwhelmed and lonely said, "I feel alone when I juggle my responsibilities as a mother and professional, and my friends are unavailable to chat. I believe we were made to connect conversationally, but our busyness secludes us." Even when she reaches out, she said, others often respond, "I'll get back to you when I can," or "Let's try to talk later." Our to-do list can often take precedence, leaving us to believe we, too, should put our feelings and needs aside and get back to work like everyone else.

Tiffany, who identified herself as a type A personality in chapter 4, says, "I'm definitely a busybody, and terrible at saying no to things, but there comes a point where filling up the calendar too much causes me to feel extremely overwhelmed. Carving out time to intentionally rest is not my forte, but when the stress from being too busy starts to intervene with my spiritual life, I know I have to re-evaluate what I'm doing and deliberately set aside times when I can focus on God's presence and rest.

"In general, I do feel that God is with me in the midst of struggles," Tiffany added. "I know if I call out to Him and pray earnestly, I will feel His comfort and presence with me. There have been moments in my life when He has felt far away, but looking back, I realize it was because I was hesitant to truly bring my struggles before Him. I know now that if I fully pour my heart out to Him, I will feel He is with me in that moment."

But it takes time to do that, doesn't it? We can't cultivate a relationship with God—or anyone else, for that matter—while running from here to there. Oh, the stress-free, peace-inducing results of being in close communion with our Maker! And many times, that involves stepping away from the busyness—and setting aside our digital devices—to get alone with our God and the people He has placed in our lives to help us process life and grow spiritually.

A TALE AS OLD AS TIME

Running down the battery, living beyond our capacity, burning the midnight oil, overextending ourselves, running on empty—regardless of the phrase you use, we've been doing it since the advent of humanity.

In Psalm 127, God told His people they didn't need to *work* more than they already did. Rather, they needed to *trust* Him more.

> Unless the Lord builds the house,
>   they labor in vain who build it;
>   unless the Lord guards the city,
>   the watchman keeps awake in vain.
>
> It is vain for you to rise up early,
>   to retire late,
>   to eat the bread of painful labors;
>   for He gives to His beloved even in his sleep
>   (verses 1-2 NASB 1995).

Wow, did you catch that? It is vain (or useless) for us to work overtime or beyond what we are able because God can provide for us even while we sleep. I can confirm, from abundant experience, that God often gives to His beloved *because* we sleep. In other words, to rest (literally) is to trust. And God always honors our trust in Him.

If we took God's promises seriously about providing for us when we are obedient to slow down and rest, we'd have many more opportunities to share life-changing conversations with our friends and family members. We'd find the more we slow down and rest rather than strive, the less lonely we are as well. By slowing down, we put ourselves in the position to sense God's presence, and we become more intentional about spending time with the people God sends our way.*

In Hebrews 10:25, we are told to not abandon our own meeting together, as is the habit of some people (and it sure is lately, isn't it?), but to encourage one another.

I don't believe the writer of Hebrews was referring only to Sunday morning services and church involvement when he told us not to forsake gathering together. I believe he was also referring to our regular meetups with other believers who encourage and sharpen us, no matter what the venue. Often, my times of accelerated spiritual growth have not been a direct result of gathering with others during a church service. Rather, my spiritual growth, personal encouragement, and enduring friendships happen most frequently when I am in small-group studies or serving others in a church ministry, or talking one-on-one with women over lunch.

Hebrews 10:25 is exhorting us to not stop meeting with those who can build us up and encourage us personally and spiritually, and to not stop meeting with those *we* can encourage as well. Close communion with like-minded individuals is essential to our spiritual growth, our victory over everyday spiritual battles, and our mental and emotional health. (I'll talk more about that in chapters 8–10.) For now, I want to address the benefits of cutting the busy and carving out space in your day to truly live again.

Sometimes we start to believe that if we're not busy *doing* something, we will be more aware of our feelings of loneliness. I know so many women who try to curb their loneliness with something more to do. One young woman told me, "If I'm not busy, I'll focus on who I don't have in my life." Oh friend, when you cut the busyness and carve out space to be alone, you can focus on Who you really *do*

---

* For more on reaping the benefits of slowing down and trusting God, see my book *When Women Long for Rest: God's Peace for Your Overwhelmed Life* (Eugene, OR: Harvest House, 2004).

have in your life, and you can follow His nudge to reconnect with
the people He knows you need around you.

GUARDING AGAINST BUSYNESS

How can you guard yourself from the loneliness and isolation of
busyness? It starts when you carve out time for what is most essential for your body, mind, and soul. Be intentional about making time
for God, yourself, and the people you know you need to invest time
in. Here's how:

1. Make Time for Rest

When I speak of rest, I'm not talking so much about getting seven
to eight hours of sleep each night (although that can do wonders to
make you less agitated, less stressed, and more healthy, and help you
enjoy your relationships more). I'm talking about scheduling times
of empty space into your day. *Every* day. Dr. Richard Swenson calls
this establishing "margin," which has made all the difference for
many people, including me. In his book *Margin: Restoring Emotional,
Physical, Financial and Time Reserves to Overloaded Lives*, Swenson,
a medical doctor, says most of the pain people experience is a result
of what he calls "the disease of marginless living."[2] Our stress, anxiety, exhaustion, unexplained physical pain, depression, and inability to function at times due to being overwhelmed comes down to
living without margin.

"The conditions of modern-day living devour margin," Swenson
writes. "If you are homeless, we send you to a shelter. If you are pen-
niless, we offer you food stamps. If you are breathless, we connect
you to oxygen. But if you are marginless, we give you yet one more
thing to do."

People who live without margin are constantly running from one
meeting or event or responsibility to another without livable space
in their lives. Dr. Swenson sees victims of marginless living enter his

office about every 15 minutes. They come to see him for pain, but don't realize their problem is they have no margin in their lives.

Margin—which is scheduled time into your day to think through issues, be creative, exercise your body, listen for God's voice in the quiet—is essential if you want to be more closely connected to God and your soul. It's also necessary to be available for the divine appointments God may bring your way, which almost always involve the presence of another person.

My margin lies in blocks of space I've created in the early mornings to protect me from the overrun, the unexpected, and the unplanned that might make me late to my appointment first thing in the morning and then running 15 to 20 minutes late the rest of the day. It's also my afternoon block of time during which I can get outside or just sit in the quiet and allow my mind to think through issues or harness creativity. Some of my most productive blocks of space (mentally and emotionally) come from walking outside near a community lake (as I talk with God) or soaking up the sun (with sunscreen on, of course) by my condo community's swimming pool as I write, read, or enjoy the quiet. Studies show being near water or "blue spaces"—whether it's a pond, fountain, waterfall, lake, the ocean, or even a swimming pool—can substantially decrease stress levels.[3] Getting away from my desk (and electronic devices) and soaking up some Vitamin D on the walking trail or near some water helps to lower (if not eliminate) my stress levels. Because stress kills and rest helps you to avoid stress, maintaining margin by scheduling blocks of rest and quiet into my day is no longer a luxury, it's an essential.

If you don't have the luxury of early morning or late afternoon blocks of empty space, be creative. Carve out a quiet time of space during your lunch hour, or when you're early to an appointment and waiting in your car, and so on. If you are intentional, you can make it happen. *You* can control your schedule rather than allowing your schedule to control you.

2. Be Intentional About Worship

Prayer, praise, and communing with God take time. But when we love God, that time passes so quickly that it hardly amounts to a task. That's because we're spending time with the One our hearts long for. In his book *A Praying Life*, Paul E. Miller wrote, "Efficiency, multitasking, and busyness all kill intimacy. In short, you can't get to know God on the fly."[4] So carve out time to simply enjoy God's presence. Worship Him on a prayer walk, spend time near nature while reflecting on His attributes, or simply sit with Him in the quiet and talk with Him as you would with the person you love the most. Miller writes, "Learning to pray doesn't offer us a less busy life; it offers us a less busy heart. In the midst of outer busyness we can develop an inner quiet. Because we are less hectic on the inside, we have a greater capacity to love..."[5] Miller's statement clarifies how busyness can leave us more lonely and less able to have fulfilling relationships with our friends and family.

3. Eliminate the Hurry

Just as we can't build a relationship with God on the fly, we can't grow closer to others in a constant state of hurry. In his book *The Ruthless Elimination of Hurry*, John Mark Comer contends that you can't fulfill God's two greatest commandments (love Him with all your heart, soul, and strength; and love your neighbor as yourself) when you're in a hurry.

"Hurry and love are incompatible," Comer observes, because "love is painfully time consuming."[6] Think about the patience and amount of time it takes to care for an older person who moves a lot slower than you, or a child who can't keep up with you. We can find that those who move slower than us can tend to annoy us. That's not love. And that kind of hurried living leaves us lonely.

In my book *When Women Long for Rest*, I wrote that, as a young mom, I realized I was being very unlike Jesus when my words to my daughter consisted of "Hurry up," "Can you move a little faster?," and "Let's go!" rather than "Be still" (Psalm 46:10 NIV), "Let's go off by ourselves to a quiet place and rest awhile" (Mark 6:31 NLT) and "Wait…" (which is all over Scripture). God never rushes His beloved. To the contrary, He is continually trying to slow us down.

Comer contrasts hurry and busyness with *patience*, the very first definition of love in 1 Corinthians 13:4-7. Slow down, guard against hurry, and love others better.

4. Practice Soul Care

As your eyes skimmed over the subhead above, you might have thought it read (or should have read) Practice Self-Care. That is, after all, most of what people are talking about these days: Self-love and self-care.

A couple years ago, I read that despite the multibillion-dollar industry that the self-care movement has created over the past decade to help women alleviate stress, we are more stressed now than before it became popular to love and care for yourself.[7] Massages, spa days, high-priced beauty products, and girlfriend getaways to Cancun or Cabo aren't lowering our stress and anxiety levels overall and making us more physically, mentally, and emotionally healthy. The article stated that self-care was inundating women with one more thing they had to do—take care of themselves for the sake of others. I believe that temporary relaxation and self-care products and services aren't getting to the crux of the real problem because we aren't taking time to cultivate our *souls*. Reinvigorating rest, absence of anxiety, and decrease in stress levels come when we start or maintain soul care—getting our minds and hearts back in touch with our Creator, the ultimate nourisher of our souls.

We are three-part beings—body, mind, and soul. Asaph said in Psalm 73:26, "God is the strength of my heart and my portion forever." *God* is the strength of our hearts. You can lower your cholesterol level and blood pressure through eating better, exercising, and reducing stress in your life. Yet even when you strengthen your *physical* heart (the organ itself) through healthy eating and exercising, you can *still* have a heart that is anxious and needs strength (and peace) from your Maker. Only He can give you strength to hope, strength to heal, strength to endure certain situations, and sustain a spiritual life in which you can encourage others.

Relaxing the body can only do so much if our hearts and minds are still anxious. Calming the mind by emptying it of thoughts is temporary; the mind can quickly fill up again with toxic thoughts, fears, and stress. God knows how to care for *every* part of us—body, mind, and soul. Allow Him to feed your spirit and soul, and the rest of your health will likely follow.

Trying to rid your life of stress and anxiety by pampering your body and mind is akin to trying to fix your car's dying engine by giving the exterior of your car a shiny new coat of paint. You and I have to commune with our Creator to get to the core of our soul and get our inner engine humming again. We need to rely on Him to fix some of those deeper issues—like why we choose to imagine and fear the future when we know He is in control of it and He has our best interests at heart. We have to spend time in the presence of our Provider to know He will provide for us in every way so we don't worry about how to make ends meet financially, or how we're going to deal with life's obstacles.

When we are convinced that God is good and will provide us with peace and rest because He loves to bless His children (Matthew 7:11), we will find it easier to chill. We should see rest as one of the most spiritual things we can do—spending quiet, unscheduled time in God's presence. Instead of getting better at chilling, we tend to be experts at *killing it*...trying to do it all ourselves and coming up empty.

EXCHANGING BUSYNESS FOR GOD TIME

If you are drawn to want to go from party to party, person to person, never wanting alone time or silence, but always wanting background noise, the television or stereo on, the noise and bluster of activity to drown out a sense of loneliness, beware. While God intends for us to live in community with one another, there is also the deep soul work He wants to do with us as we get alone with Him. A Christ-follower cannot live and grow while in isolation from others, but she also cannot live without that quietness of the soul, that alone time with Christ, that is required to gain the character and spiritual strength that only He can give us.

Strength is not in bluster and noise. Strength is in quietness. The lake must be calm if the heavens are to be reflected on its surface...Every life that would be strong must have its Holy of Holies into which only God enters.[8]

Taking time to be alone with God isn't to rid ourselves of guilt feelings for not doing what we feel we're supposed to do as believers. It is much more than that, my friend. It is the start of a closer *relationship* with the Living God.

THE POSITIVE IMPACT
OF TIME WITH GOD

Here are some other ways time with God can positively impact your life.

It improves our attitude and perspective.

When we get alone with God and His Word, our minds are renewed and our focus switches from ourselves and how lonely we are to embracing the alone times with God and the richness that comes through them. It can also increase our faith in Who He is and all He can do. Our faith and trust in God is only as strong as our knowledge of Him. And spending time with God to know what He's like—and looking for Him to show up everywhere in answer to our prayers—can be life changing.

> Our faith and trust in God is only
> as strong as our knowledge of Him.

Alexa, the young mom I referred to in the introduction and in chapter 2, told me, "I am particularly lonely when I'm feeling like I should be doing *more* every day, like cleaning, and spending time with God. Also, when I don't take the time to emotionally unpack things and instead shove them down, the emotions continue to bubble up and cause me to feel overwhelmed."

"But," Alexa admits, "I need to stop making excuses for why I'm too busy to spend time with God. I have the time; I just prefer to spend it doing something else. But when I spend consistent time with Him, He reveals Himself profoundly and in beautiful ways."

It accentuates the difference between our faith and the world's cynicism.

Have you ever spent time with God in prayer and emerged from that time with a reinforced belief that He can do the impossible? Time in God's presence changes us. It makes us more like Jesus. It strengthens our faith so it can stand against the cynicism in this world. If you have a growing doubt over Who God is and what He can accomplish, it's likely you haven't spent enough time with Him lately. And if you have a friend who is deconstructing her faith and questioning everything about what she's been taught all her life, it's possible she, too, is not in the Word of God and experiencing His character, but listening to what secular psychology and this culture is telling her, not what Jesus said and reinforced.

It increases our confidence in who we are.

When we set aside busyness (and the cynicism of everyone else in the world) and spend time getting to know God, we end up finding out not only Who He is and what He's capable of, but who *we* are and what we're capable of doing with His power and strength.

David spent much time alone with God and the sheep, drawing upon God's strength to kill a lion and a bear before downing a giant—all when he was likely still a teenager. And that same David, who knew alone time with God, confidently said,

> By You I can run at a troop of warriors;
> and by my God I can leap over a wall (Psalm 18:29).

WHAT IS MOST IMPORTANT?

We can cut the busyness from our lives when we know what is most important to us. (By the way, I just wrote *busymess* by mistake, but that's certainly a concept to ponder, isn't it?) In his book *Essentialism: The Disciplined Pursuit of Less,* Greg McKeown writes:

> There are far more activities and opportunities in the world than we have time and resources to invest in. And although many of them may be good or even very good, the fact is that most are trivial and few are vital. The way of the Essentialist involves learning to tell the difference—learning to filter through all those options and selecting only those that are truly essential.[9]

Can you imagine how becoming an essentialist might impact your schedule and your feelings of being overwhelmed? If you knew you were sticking to what is essential, you would experience fewer questions and less uncertainty about your purpose, and I believe far less loneliness because you would be living more intentionally.

McKeown continues:

> Essentialism is not about how to get more things done; it's about how to get the *right* things done. It doesn't mean just doing less for the sake of less either. It is about making the wisest possible investment of your time and energy in order to operate at our highest point of contribution by doing only what is essential.[10]

McKeown calls the way of the Essentialist "living by design, not by default."[11]

When you and I know who we are (loved creations of God), and why we're here (to love God with all our heart, soul, mind, and strength, and love our neighbor as ourselves), we can strive toward only what is essential in order to fulfill God's purpose for us. That means making time for God *and* people, but in ways that provide the highest point of contribution—to their lives and ours.

Solid, healthy relationships take time. And if we feel we don't have the time, or the relationships, we are likely filling our schedules with opportunities rather than essential activities and responsibilities that move us toward God's desired purpose for us.

What is essential in *your* life? Is it your career or personal achievements? A sense of productivity? Your marriage? Your children? Your walk with God? Your extended family? Your image? Your friendships with those who can encourage your spiritual growth and help propel you forward? Sharing the gospel with others? When you know what's essential, you will find your no to what's not.

KEEP YOURSELF BALANCED

Make sure you're balanced in the amount of time you spend with God (in prayer and worship, letting His peace pour into your life, being in His Word), with self (through exercise, rest, play, creativity through hobbies or projects, quiet times to think deeply and reflect, time to read and grow personally), and with others (whose lives we can build into and whom we can allow to build into ours). If you find you don't have room for one or all of those three areas, look at your schedule and ask yourself, *What can go? What is not so important? What is preventing me from getting to the place where God wants me to be?*

As you cut the busyness and carve out time to be with God, you will find yourself more attuned to His voice and more available for His divine appointments, which will replace your loneliness with deeper, more fulfilling relationships with God and others.

BEING INTENTIONAL

1. Read the following verses and record next to each one what God does as you rest.

   Psalm 4:8:

   Psalm 127:1-2 (NASB):

2. According to Matthew 11:28-29, who invites you to rest and let Him do the heavy lifting?

3. What does Psalm 121:2-4 say God never does?

4. Isaiah 30:15 says, "In repentance and rest you will be saved, in quietness and trust is your strength." What do you think this means?

5. Which of the four ways to make time for rest (on pages 120-124) do you most need to practice?

What are some ways you can gift yourself with space this week? (Think outside the box of work and/or responsibilities at home and find practical ways to make it happen.)

A CHALLENGE TO HELP YOU GROW

We make time to do what is most important to us. Create a plan for how you will become more balanced in your work and personal life by incorporating time with God, time for yourself, and time with others.

I will add God to my day and week by:

I will add extra space for personal time by:

I will add friendship time to my life by:

CHAPTER 6

THE LONELINESS OF MISTRUST

Allowing Yourself to Be Transparent

To love at all is to be vulnerable…Love anything and your heart will certainly be wrung and possibly broken. If you want to make sure of keeping it intact, you must give your heart to no one. Wrap it carefully with hobbies and little luxuries, avoid all entanglements, lock it safe in a casket of your own selfishness, there it will not be broken. It will become unbreakable, impenetrable, irredeemable.[1]

UNKNOWN

Several years ago, I received a hurtful voice message from a friend I trusted. To this day, it's still difficult to describe the pain I felt that day as her words pierced my heart. In that moment, I remember feeling that I never wanted to get close to anyone else again. I never wanted to *hurt* that way again.

I wish I could tell you that I have never been hurt like that since. But in the high-tech world we live in, others can hurt us even more easily today through

- a careless or painful comment on social media,

- an email fired off as an emotional reaction and then sent before the writer took time to carefully read it over and soften it,

- or an impulsive text message in which someone vented and pressed *send* before thinking about how their words would come across.

A broken heart can hurt intensely. And betrayal, in any number of ways, can shatter us, whether in person or through a screen. But to feel the hurt of betrayal means we first had to love and extend our heart to someone. Our hearts were never meant to be untouched, unmoved, or unloved. To love another, and trust another, is certainly a risk. And today I know that anything worthwhile, and every priceless experience, involves some degree of risk.

But why do we instinctively think that never trusting again means we'll never get hurt?

After decades of ministering to women, I've discovered we tend to respond the way we do out of a desire to protect ourselves from further pain. *If friendships hurt, I don't need them anymore. If risking my heart and opening myself up to others and making myself vulnerable results in this kind of pain or rejection, I'm done with relationship building. I'm fine on my own.*

But we're not fine. We are nursing pain. And in some cases, our own pride and ego. And we are only hurting ourselves by thinking we can continue life's journey without the people God has brought into our lives to help us through.

When we can lay aside ego and seek to love others as God intends them to be loved, and trust them in the form of giving them another chance *not* to hurt us (as God does with us, even though He knows we will still fail Him at times), we are getting closer to understanding His intention for godly, unselfish relationships in the body of Christ.

Trust may be difficult for you. At times, it might feel impossible—especially if a parent abandoned you, a spouse walked out on you, or a close friend betrayed you. Maybe you've even experienced all three.

From my own experiences, as well as the stories of countless other women I've talked with through the years, I'm convinced we can't fully trust others until we have learned to fully trust God. Not all people are fully trust*worthy*, but God certainly is.

OUR EXPERIENCE WITH MISTRUST

I realize there are many reasons you might be hesitant to trust others or make yourself vulnerable in a friendship. Maybe you once confided in someone, and they used what you told them about yourself as a reason for backing away from you or ending the friendship. Perhaps you've learned through experience not to trust someone until they have proven themselves trustworthy. It is easier to *not* trust, *not* give someone our hearts, and just wait for the betrayal to happen, and when it does, feel relieved that we weren't that invested. But really, is that any way to live? I'm so thankful God doesn't hold back that way with us, even though He knows what our weaknesses are and the next time we'll disappoint Him. Instead of exercising caution with us, He continues to love us unconditionally. Some even say He loves us recklessly. You and I can learn a lot from God's perfect love toward us when it comes to extending our love and friendship to others, even when they've hurt us.

For the first 40 years of my life, I immediately and instinctively trusted people, unless I had a clear indication to do otherwise. I was often called naïve. Or gullible. Or too trusting. There have been times I've been around a person who I now know is toxic, and I continued to give them the benefit of the doubt that they had changed and next time things would go differently. I believed it was always best to extend grace rather than be suspicious or critical. But my sister shared with me this ancient wisdom you may have read or heard as well: The definition of insanity is doing the same thing over and over and expecting different results.

Just because we determine to give someone the benefit of the doubt and trust them doesn't make them trustworthy. Just because we love them unconditionally and continue to extend grace toward them doesn't necessarily make them rise to the occasion and treat us better. Put simply, *more of the same doesn't mean change will happen.* I know today that God's Spirit can give us wisdom and discernment in exercising *caution* toward others (not pessimism, skepticism, or cynicism), and a quiet heart that waits for the Holy Spirit's direction when it comes to whom we trust with more of ourselves.

FRIENDSHIPS CAN BE COMPLICATED

Friendships can be wonderful. But friendships can also become complicated or difficult at times because people can become complicated and difficult at times. You may come up against a person who is dealing with issues (or not dealing with them) and get pulled into their drama and dysfunction. And sometimes it's *your* wounds and idiosyncrasies at play. There are also times when the wounds and dysfunctions of both you and your friend are causing strain on the relationship.

Think about your friendships through the years. If your friendship journey is anything like most everyone else's, then you have likely had a friend who competed with you to the point that you didn't have the energy to continue with that relationship. You have likely had a friend who betrayed you through gossip or going out with your boyfriend, or stealing your idea and taking credit for it, and that made you not want to trust anyone else. Perhaps you lost a friend quickly and without warning through a sudden move, an unexpected death, a deep hurt or betrayal, or some sort of misunderstanding that resulted in their rejection of you and you didn't get a chance to explain or try to make the situation right. Any of those factors can make any woman not want to give her heart to anyone else again. These kinds of experiences can make you wonder if something is intrinsically wrong with you because you're unable to keep friendships. Or they can make you feel you're better off having friendships with men only because women—even Christian women—can be so petty and catty and competitive.

Perhaps you've also had a friend—or two—who...

> needed more from you than you could provide
>
> betrayed a confidence or gossiped about you to another friend
>
> became jealous of you and dropped you
>
> backed away from you because of your intensity or passion (for God, perhaps?)
>
> was wounded emotionally and ended up wounding you

People who hurt will hurt people. People who are wounded often wound others. We can even do these same things to others without realizing it. A bad experience with someone doesn't amount to giving up trust and friendships altogether. When we can view others' wounds and insecurities with compassion, we can more readily realize we have many of the same wounds, and we can love them as Jesus does.

ESTABLISH YOUR FOUNDATION

Dear friend, people will always let us down. But when we build our lives, hopes, and expectations on Jesus, the Solid Rock, that firm foundation won't collapse when a friendship or marriage does. A foundation built on Christ will hold firm, allowing us to love and trust people as God guides, and as He provides wisdom and discernment for our relationships and sometimes the freedom to love some from a distance so they don't crush our hearts again.

If you are hesitant about opening up, becoming transparent, and trusting others, you are not alone. All of us have been wounded. Everyone has experienced betrayal at some point or another. You are not the only one who has been taken advantage of, deceived, blindsided, manipulated, or treated badly. These things happen because we live among people who don't know better. And sometimes they do know better, yet because of their sinful nature, they do it anyway.

I want you to live and experience *every* relationship in your life from a position of courage and confidence, knowing Who truly loves you and Who can work all things for good—despite how your parent, sibling, spouse, child, or friend is behaving. You can gain the courage to trust again when you rest in God's goodness, knowing that as you extend yourself toward others, He sees it all and ultimately has your back.

When we cement in our minds that Jesus is the Only One who will never disappoint, He can empower us to leave our misgivings behind and forge into new friendships with others and be more effective representatives, ambassadors, and witnesses of Him in a hurting world where people will continue to disappoint. A deeper trust in God as your firm and never-shifting foundation will help you be at ease when becoming transparent and starting to trust others.

A deeper trust in God as your firm and never-shifting foundation will help you be at ease when becoming transparent and starting to trust others.

OUR HESITANCY TO TRUST

We all want to be seen and understood by others. But sometimes we hesitate to put ourselves out there so we *can* be seen. Sometimes we tend to erect walls and hide behind facades and then we lament our loneliness, which occurs because others don't really know us. I realize this is often the result of trust issues.

One of my friends shared with me about a young woman who came to her house recently and told her how very lonely she was. This woman was single, involved in her church and community, and was a people person.

"And yet she's lonely," my friend said, surprised. But this woman also admitted, "I just don't share everything about my life with people." Thankfully, that precious lonely woman asked my friend to become her accountability partner because "she realized she needs to be transparent and connect deeper."

Sometimes we are lonely because we aren't allowing others to see enough of ourselves to where we feel known. We haven't become transparent. And when we share our lives with others we can trust, we make it possible to experience more intimate friendships. But we must know what to be transparent about.

THE RELATIONAL RISKS OF TRANSPARENCY

In my early years of ministry, I had a business arrangement with a woman I came to trust and consider as a friend. We worked together for several years until the morning I received an email from her informing me that she was no longer interested in working with me. At all. She referred to something I had shared with her in a previous conversation and had concluded that my work ethic wasn't as strong as hers. That hurt me not only because I was losing her help at a time when I still needed it, but because I felt she had used some personal information against me that I trusted her with. I also felt I lost a friend.

Looking back now, I realize I never should have been that dependent on her. Anytime you and I depend too much on others, we take a risk that they will disappoint us in one way or another. I should have trusted that just as God brought her to me when I most needed help, He would provide someone else in her absence once she wanted to break ties.

It's difficult when others misunderstand or judge us for something that is not necessarily wrong, but merely different. We all have values we consider important and core to who we are. But they will differ from person to person, even in the body of Christ. (More about that in chapter 9.)

Through the years, whenever that friend comes to mind, a part of my heart still hurts. I wish that the relationship could have continued at least on a friendship level. But God sometimes brings people in and out of our lives for reasons and for seasons. And people change or grow or digress during those seasons. So it's wise for us to recognize that not all friendships, work relationships, and "contacts" are necessarily meant to be in our lives long term. God sometimes allows certain relationships to end so He can bring us to the next ones that will move us closer to where He wants us.

After I lost that friend, an author friend of mine referred me to a young man she was working with who ended up working for me as well. That young man was able to help me take my ministry to the next level. I also discovered that by working with him, the dynamic of hurt feelings, assumptions, judgments, annoyances, touchy feelings, and "are we still friends?" component that is often present among women was completely absent. I have never had to wonder what this young man was *really* thinking. He gets the work done. And now he's a friend as well. That entire experience of losing one business associate and gaining another made me realize that sometimes when one friendship or working relationship ends, it's because God plans to replace it with something better suited for us. It also made me a lot more cautious about how much information I share and with whom.

JESUS UNDERSTANDS

Jesus was no stranger to betrayal and abandonment by those He was closest to while on this earth. He was constantly being disappointed by those who claimed to love Him but misunderstood Him or were disillusioned by His actions. Yet He never stopped loving them and giving them chances to grow in their trust. We can be sure He considered their brokenness, their sinful nature, their inability to do anything good apart from Him. He considers ours too.

Psalm 9:10 tells us, "Those who know Your name will put their trust in You, for You, LORD, have not abandoned those who seek You." Notice this verse is not in the future tense as if it's a promise of what's to come. Sometimes we have a difficult time trusting promises. We prefer to have our assurance in hand already. This verse does not say, "You, Lord, *will not* abandon those who seek You." The psalmist is writing in hindsight about what God has *already* done for those who know Him and put their trust in Him. You've probably heard the phrase "God has already gone before you and knows exactly what's ahead." Well, because He has gone before You, He can credibly say He has not forsaken or abandoned you. God, in going before you, has already provided your comfort, your hope, your deliverance, your salvation. We have only to trust His Word. Second Corinthians 1:20 tells us all of God's promises are fulfilled, and even though you may not see it yet in your present or future, whatever you are going through or will go through is already past tense to Him because He has not abandoned those who seek Him.

EXERCISE DISCERNMENT
BEFORE TRUSTING

The older we become, the more we may realize that truly good friends are difficult to find. The majority of women I surveyed for this book, regardless of their age, told me that they don't know how to find a friend they can trust. They often find it difficult to open up, to take the time to form relationships, to spend the time it takes in a conversation and go deeper and discover new things about themselves and others. It doesn't help that our high-tech, social media-driven world reinforces that text is more efficient than talk, acquaintances are the equivalent of friendships, and conversations must be brief or you will be rudely inconveniencing someone by taking up their time.

So many women feel at a loss when it comes to finding iron-sharpening friendships. We often tell ourselves "I'll find them at church," but turning to the person next to you and saying "Hi" during the greeting time at a church service isn't enough to start a friendship. Getting into a small group, joining a Bible study, sharing prayer requests, and any other situation that opens the door to being real with one another—those are the ways trusting friendships start and develop.

Some friendships are for a season and your season with someone may be past—and your season with another friend may be just beginning. I would caution you to pray for discernment when it comes to who you get close to, who to be transparent with, and who to let in a little closer. We don't have to be best friends with everyone. But you and I need a few close friends or mentors with whom we can be ourselves. Trust goes both ways. As you open your life before others and trust them, they may open themselves up and trust you in return. But it helps to ask God for His wisdom and discernment when it comes to letting someone into your heart a little further.

Proverbs 12:26 tells us, "The righteous choose their friends carefully" (NIV). In my book *Drama Free*, I included a section describing the five kinds of friends every woman needs. I believe the descriptions for two of them are worth repeating here so that you cannot only know the kinds of friends to *look* for and trust, but the kind of friend to *be* as well.

- *The faithful friend* is the one who is there for you through thick and thin and doesn't keep track of how many times she has called you versus how many times you have taken the initiative to call her. She will never talk behind your back and will always pick up where the two of you left off. She is dependable and you never have to question her loyalty.

- *The faith-filled friend* is the one who reminds you to trust in the Lord instead of worrying or becoming anxious, and who fills your tank and leaves you feeling more energized and stronger by being in her presence. She is also a great fine-tuning friend who speaks the truth to you in love with the goal of helping you stay spiritually strong. She will most likely love you as Jesus does—without condition.

If you have a friend who meets both of these qualities, she is a rarity. Hold on to her and strive to be for her what she needs in you as well. If you have these qualities covered in a few different friends, you are richer than you thought. And if you still long to have these kinds of friends at this point, start asking God to make you a faithful and faith-filled friend for someone else. That's often how these types of friendships start.

LEARNING TO TRUST AGAIN

It's possible one of your friends now could very well be your faithful or faith-filled friend. Maybe you just haven't given her a chance to know you more fully. Or, perhaps God is preparing you now for a friend you will soon meet. Here are some ways you can begin to become more vulnerable with others. As you trust God more, you'll become more comfortable with trusting others.

1. Look at others through the lens of grace.

As I mentioned in chapter 2, we're all broken. That means every person has their weaknesses, faults, idiosyncrasies, emotional triggers, and tendencies to sin. Thus, getting to know someone means getting to see their damage. But grace is the glue that holds you two together. Remember, you are broken too, and that may give you more compassion toward others and help you see them through the lens of grace.

2. Lower your expectations as a way of extending grace.

No one is perfect but Jesus. So, if you're a perfectionist, you'd be wise to lower your expectations in order to decrease your disappointment level. Even if you aren't a perfectionist, it's still wise to lower your expectations, including when it comes to your husband, children, friends, boss, and anyone you might think highly of. In fact, lower your expectations of your favorite podcaster, your favorite Christian speaker or author, and your pastor too. We are all human. We all mess up at times. Yes, the standard is held higher for some in ministry. But that doesn't mean we never sin or disappoint someone. Give those you love and admire—and those you don't love and admire—a break. Extend grace to others by lowering your expectations. When you don't expect as much from others—in a sincere, noncynical way—you will be less likely to trust them carelessly or invest too much in the relationship to the point you feel burned, devastated, or rejected if they act or react a certain way.

I'm definitely not suggesting you eliminate or compromise on your standards. Just lower the expectation of another's response or actions where and when appropriate, as a means of extending God's grace toward another sinner saved by grace.

3. Learn to filter your words.

If you tend to be a talker like me, you may have learned by now to err on the side of caution rather than exposure, simply because some people don't need to know everything. Your friend, family member, or colleague doesn't need to know what you're thinking at certain times, or even those feelings that you've just discussed with God. When you filter your words, you have less at stake when someone betrays a confidence or carelessly lets something slip. I've taken this concept further by telling myself to "filter your words with love" when talking with certain individuals who take offense more easily, or with whom I might tend to be blunt.

4. Limit your verbal engagement if you see it's not working.

Talking through an issue isn't always the most effective or even the most appreciated thing to do when dealing with certain personality types or situations. Even when we have good intentions, like wanting to clear up a matter with someone, or wanting to reopen a situation to establish trust again, it can backfire on us, depending on who we are dealing with.

I have learned through the years that just because I initiated communication or meant well doesn't mean I'm always right. Just because I'm sincerely trying to make things better with my words or explanation doesn't mean I am. Take your hurt or offense to God first and ask Him if it's worth bringing up with someone else, or if He wants to do the healing on your heart because He knows the other person involved won't understand or isn't receptive. When we go to God first rather than rushing ahead on our own, we give the devil less of an opportunity to divide us through unintentional words and unfortunate responses and reactions.

TRUST THE RECONCILER
OF ALL THINGS

When I received that hurtful voice message I mentioned at the beginning of this chapter, I initially tried to repair the relationship with words—first, a humble phone call, and then a follow-up card in the mail reminding the person that I loved her and I was available when she was ready to talk. In both cases, she remained silent. It was difficult for me (almost agonizing) to step back, wait for God to work, and not continue to try to repair the situation with an excess of words. But I knew God could be trusted, so I relied on Him to speak His gentle voice to my heart and hers. I knew I could trust Him to work where I couldn't.

After a period of waiting (and prayer), she expressed a desire to meet and talk. And all I could think was, *That was You, God. Because I ran out of ways to make this right.*

She and I got through that difficulty and learned much about ourselves and each other in the process. Today, we are still in touch. That is a result of God's Spirit of reconciliation. You and I don't have the ability, within our good intentions and relationship skills alone, to grow closer to someone else through a difficulty or offense or a deep hurt. And we don't have the ability on our own to leave the hurt with our Lord and trust again unless we trust the Reconciler and the God of second chances. Only the Spirit of God can soften hearts, clear up misunderstandings, and reveal the truth to us. And what a learning experience we receive in trusting the Reconciler of All Things to do the work that we cannot!

WHEN GOD IS IN THE MIX

I truly believe for friendships to develop and last, God must be at the center. As two people continue to grow in their love for and obedience to Christ, the friendship will continue to grow too. If we keep that common goal of growing in our relationship with Christ and remain women who forgive and extend grace freely, what can separate us? When we do that, God's love will cement the bond. For this reason, family ties between those in the body of Christ can be stronger than family ties through birth or household. Sometimes there's less damage among sisters in Christ than blood sisters. It all comes down to our heart and our willingness to forgive and keep extending.

For friendships to develop and last,
God must be at the center.

Missionary Amy Carmichael said these powerful words in her classic book *If*:

> If I do not give a friend "the benefit of the doubt," but put the worst construction instead of the best on what is said or done, then I know nothing of Calvary love.[2]

Can you practice Calvary love toward those who hurt you or those you might otherwise want to avoid from now on? Can you treat a friend like Jesus would when they betray your trust because you realize you are capable of doing the same thing? Christ continues to give us chance after chance, knowing we'll never get it absolutely right on this side of heaven. Perhaps it's time for you to take another chance, make yourself vulnerable, and trust God to hold your heart and have your back as you build your trust in others and forge your way into deeper friendships.

BEING INTENTIONAL

1. There is much wisdom in Scripture about how to choose and keep friends. Read the following verses and record next to each one Scripture's warning or guideline concerning friendships.

Proverbs 10:18-19:

Proverbs 12:17:

Proverbs 12:18:

Proverbs 15:18:

Proverbs 17:9:

Proverbs 18:24:

Proverbs 20:19:

Proverbs 22:24:

1 Corinthians 15:33:

2. Explain how establishing your foundation on Jesus can better help you develop friendships with others.

3. How can exercising discernment about who to trust improve your friendship experience and decrease your disappointment level?

4. Which of the four ways of "Learning to Trust Again" (see pages 144-145) would be most helpful to you right now and why?

5. How can you start practicing it daily?

A CHALLENGE TO HELP YOU GROW

In chapter 3, I asked you who you might want to open up to about your struggles. It's time to ask that person, if you haven't already, to be your faith-filled friend. Pray about it this week, then talk with that person. Record in the space below how that went and what your plan is from here on out to accept that friend's fine-tuning help. If the person says no, continue to pray and seek the Lord's guidance. If you're not involved in a small group or class at your church, join one. The more connected you are in your church, the more you're likely to find a faith-filled friend.

CHAPTER 7

THE LONELINESS
OF #MEFIRST

Preparing Yourself to Love Again

Dying to yourself doesn't mean missing out on true
life; it means embracing life as it was always meant to
be—worshiping God, serving others, and living for his
glory. Dying to yourself isn't the loss of who you are as a
person; it's discovering who you were meant to be—a
servant, a sacrifice, and a recipient of God's grace.[1]

GRETCHEN SAFFLES

One of the reasons we tend to keep others at a distance is because
we live in a society that constantly reinforces the value of "me first."
Protect yourself at all costs.

Do you.

You are the single most important person in your life.

I'm sure you've also been told you control your own story. But *do*
you? Or does the sovereign God of the Universe control all things,
including your story? And can He redeem it and restore it and cause
all things to work together in it to make you more like His Son?
(Romans 8:28-29).

Many cultural sayings right now sound good. But they're not biblical. And they are not what Jesus taught.

Anyone on earth can offer advice, whether they have wisdom or not. And if we're desperate enough, we will take what someone says simply because it's input. Or it makes us feel good. But how very dangerous it is to do that.

Scripture tells us the wisdom of the world is foolishness to God, just as the wisdom of God is seen as foolishness to the world (1 Corinthians 1:25). God is incapable of being foolish, of course. But to the world, His wisdom appears as nonsense. Yet according to God, the wisdom of the world is clear and utter foolishness.

There is a difference between advice and wisdom. Advice can come from Google, your grandmother, or a stranger sitting next to you at Taco Bell. But wisdom comes only from God, or from those who are familiar with His Word, because God is the source of wisdom. Know the difference between opinion, well-meaning advice, and godly and biblical wisdom.

For example, self-love is a very popular movement right now. But it does not lead to the more abundant and fulfilling life that Jesus offered. It also does not lead to an ability to love others well. In the end, it's a recipe for deep loneliness.

Recently, I saw a woman wearing a sweatshirt that proclaimed, "I love me." I also saw a hashtag on social media that almost made me laugh if it wasn't so very sad: #selfloveismynewrelationship.

I've heard many believers say that Jesus taught self-love. Their proof text is Matthew 22:39, where Jesus said the second greatest commandment is that "you shall love your neighbor as yourself." They argue that Jesus was endorsing self-love by commanding us to love others as much as we should love ourselves. But unlike the world's idea of loving self *so that* you can love others, Jesus taught the contrary: We are to love others as much as we *already* love ourselves. He knew self-preference was natural, and preferring others with a sacrificial, selfless love was contrary to human nature. Jesus' words in Matthew 22:39 were not a command to love ourselves first and others second. Rather, He made it clear the only way we can love others appropriately and selflessly and as God loved us is to put ourselves aside *in order to* love others.

SELF-LOVE VERSUS SELF-CARE

Not only is there a difference between advice and wisdom, there is also a difference between self-love and self-care. Self-*care* is biblical. Scripture tells us our bodies are the temple of the Lord and therefore we are to treat our bodies with reverence, respect, and care, as we would the dwelling place of God (1 Corinthians 6:19-20). That certainly does not imply we are to worship ourselves and put ourselves above everyone else. Rather, we are to keep ourselves pure, holy, and healthy because the Spirit of God lives within us.

Self-*love*, on the other hand, implies self-preference, putting ourselves first, and loving ourselves more. Jesus never taught that. He taught us to pick up our cross and die to self (our preferences and desires) in order to love and serve others. He modeled sacrificial love. If Jesus wanted to demonstrate self-love, He would have never set His face toward the cross. He would have protected His life over ours. He would have never fulfilled God's mission for Him. Scripture tells us that "for the joy set before Him [Jesus] endured the cross, despising the shame" and sealed our redemption (Hebrews 12:3). He set aside Himself to rescue us. Self-love and humility (James 4:10) are at complete odds with each other.

Yet many believers have jumped onto this culture's bandwagon that purports if we do not *love* ourselves, we *loathe* ourselves. When Jesus made a reference to that extreme, He was using a contrast to show us how very much we should love *Him*. In Luke 14:26, Jesus said, "If you want to be my disciple, you must, by comparison, hate everyone else—your father and mother, wife and children, brothers and sisters—yes, even your own life. Otherwise, you cannot be my disciple" (NLT). That's how intensely He wanted us to love Him.

And when we love Him above all else, we will know how to love others and care for ourselves as He desires.

Jesus' reference for us to hate ourselves and love others was never a command to literally hate, despise, or injure ourselves in any way. He was telling us to disregard our preferences and our fleshly desires that naturally want only what's best for us, and to prefer one another in love (Romans 12:10).

The world teaches "love yourself." Jesus taught "love others." The world teaches "You are number one. You are the single most important person in your world." Jesus taught God is first (ever and always), others are second, and self is last. That's the way of the cross. That's the way of sacrificial, selfless love.

When you and I understand the danger and inherent destructiveness of a me-first mentality, we will quickly embrace God's way of doing things. We will set aside our personal preferences so we can humbly serve others in the name of Jesus. That is the true gospel of Jesus Christ. And loving God first, others second, and ourselves last is a prescription for a lonely-free life as well.

> Loving God first, others second, and ourselves
> last is a prescription for a lonely-free life.

SIFTING THROUGH THE DAMAGE

Now, if what I just wrote makes you upset because you have already put yourself aside out of a desire to love and serve others and yet were manipulated or abused, please hear me out. Dear sister, I am not saying you don't matter and that you should let anyone treat you any way they want. I am not saying you are to *ever* let someone abuse you. Jesus never taught that. He loves you as His precious child and His heart hurts when your desire to love and serve is trampled upon by others. Be assured that God is just, and He will deal with whomever has dealt with you in hurtful, damaging ways. I'm asking you now to trust that the God who created you to serve and love others will protect your heart as you wisely invest in the friendships and relationships He brings your way.

Sometimes we are blindsided when someone who seemed so wonderful turns on us and betrays our trust. But that doesn't mean it is a mistake to trust others or to love them unconditionally. Rather, it is because such people have been damaged and wrecked by sin, and have allowed themselves to be a tool of the enemy to try to hurt you.

(If you are struggling with the wounds of physical or sexual abuse, please see the book *Hope for Healing from Domestic Abuse*, which was written by my friend Karen DeArmond Gardner, a survivor of domestic abuse *within* the church. Her personal story, which includes biblical insights and practical steps to help you find hope and healing, will encourage your heart and help you find your place today as a woman willing to love again. Karen understands far more than I ever will about what you may have experienced, and her words will pour a healing salve on your soul. You can find Karen's book at AnotherOneFree.com.[2])

My friend, please start praying about your willingness and ability to set yourself aside and trust God that as you seek to serve others (in *nonabusive* relationships), He will watch your back. I am convinced that when we practice dying to self for the cause of Jesus, God will care for us mentally, emotionally, and spiritually. It doesn't mean we'll never get hurt. Those assurances don't exist as long as we walk this sin-infested planet. Rather, it means God will be with you, guiding you, giving you discernment, and making you more like Jesus in whatever happens as a result of your obedience to Him.

SACRIFICIAL LOVE
INSTEAD OF SELF-LOVE

The self-love tidal wave has swept over our culture—and some of our churches—and left us drenched with delusion. There is no fulfillment in self-love. Finding the best version of yourself is elusive, ever-fleeting, and not possible apart from the Holy Spirit's transformation in your life. Again, Jesus never taught self-love. Instead, He demonstrated Calvary love.

Our culture continues to be obsessed with self-love—so much so that the church has bought into it too, with Christian celebrities posting selfies and jumping on the #MeFirst campaign as if it were the most emotionally healthy thing we can do.

But putting ourselves first is not our key to happiness or fulfillment. It is not the secret to being mentally and emotionally healthy. It is a recipe for deeper loneliness because love of self never satisfies. To the contrary, love for God and others (in that order)—the way God intended—always brings fulfillment.

DETHRONING EGO

The biggest relationship killer today is not irreconcilable differences. It is not betrayal or mistrust. It is not a lack of communication and honesty. The biggest relationship killer, hands down, is ego—our own and that of others. It is from our ego that subsequent sins flow and end up being the last brick that toppled the marriage or friendship. Because we cannot control, comfort, or otherwise manipulate someone else's ego, we must address our own.

In chapter 4, when I was addressing our sense of inadequacy, I quoted from Timothy Keller's book *The Freedom of Self-Forgetfulness*. Keller's words are worth repeating here in this chapter on the loneliness of putting self first:

> The ego often hurts. That is because it has something incredibly wrong with it. Something unbelievably wrong with it. It is *always* drawing attention to itself—it does so every single day. It is always making us think about how we look and how we are treated. People sometimes say

their feelings are hurt. But our *feelings* can't be hurt. It is the ego that hurts—my sense of self, my identity. Our feelings are fine! It is my ego that hurts.[3]

BECOMING SELF-AWARE

Do you know what it's like to be talking and have someone suddenly hush you because "You're talking *so* loud"? Granted, that often came from my teenager who was embarrassed by just about anything I'd do or say, but eventually, as she got over the embarrassed-at-everything stage, I began to realize her observations were sometimes true. The sudden humiliating feeling of realizing I was being boisterous or way too loud was a good impetus for me to start becoming more aware of my volume—both audibly and in terms of the number of words I use.

My daughter, a millennial (the generation of individuals born between 1981 and 1996) and a manager over several millennials and Gen Zs (those born between 1997 and 2012), often talks about the negative professional and relational consequences of those who are not self-aware. And it's not only a problem with her generation and those younger. It's an issue that affects anyone who has a me-first mentality.

To be self-aware, according to Merriam-Webster, is to have an awareness of one's own personality or individuality.

In an article titled "The Importance of Self-Awareness," the writer defined self-awareness as "the ability to tune in to your own feelings, thoughts, and actions. When people are self-aware, they understand their strengths and challenges and know what helps them thrive. They also understand that how they see themselves may be different from how others see them."[4]

That last line is key. When we have a me-first mentality, we often have no awareness of how we are coming across and how others are perceiving our selfishness or sense of entitlement.

Scripture teaches us a mindset that's very contrary to a me-first mentality and lifestyle.

We are taught to die to self and to desires that are contrary to Christ's. Paul, the apostle, spelled out what this looks like in his letter to the Galatians:

> I have been crucified with Christ; and it is no longer I who live, but Christ lives in me; and the life which I now live in the flesh I live by faith in the Son of God, who loved me and gave Himself up for me (2:20).

That Scripture verse is encouraging us to die to our fleshly desires and old self and to let Christ live through us so we exhibit *His* characteristics—the fruit of the Spirit—rather than the fruit of our fleshly impulses. Galatians 5:22-23 lists the fruit of the Spirit, or characteristics of living under the Spirit's control: love, joy, peace, patience, kindness, goodness, faithfulness, gentleness, and self-control.

When we yield to the Spirit's control rather than assume the throne of our life, we will exhibit these characteristics of Christ's, not self. And the beauty of Galatians 2:20 is this: Through the death of self comes new life within us that is empowered by Jesus, *who loved us and gave Himself for us.* Look at the last part of that verse again. Paul isn't saying his motivation is to escape the fiery pit of hell. He isn't saying he is grudgingly dying to self. For him, it is a joy and way of life and tribute to "the Son of God, *who loved me and gave Himself up for me.*" To Paul, it is *personal* that his life not be personally *his*, but the Lord's.

Oswald Chambers said, "Our Lord's teaching was always *anti*-self realization. His purpose is not the development of a person. His purpose is to make a person exactly like Himself, and the Son of God is characterized by self-expenditure."[5]

Paul's goal was to become a perfected representation of his loving Savior, Jesus.

Being self-aware can help us recognize whether we're acting from a me-first mentality or a Jesus mentality. Someone who is not self-aware is loud while everyone else is thinking, *Why is she talking so loud?* Someone who is not self-aware enters a room and makes everything all about herself, while she passes that off as an outgoing, loud, or extroverted personality. Someone who is not self-aware is not conscientious of others' feelings, fears, or insecurities, and violates boundaries verbally, physically, and emotionally. Someone who is not self-aware can also be the downer in the room because she's projecting her negativity or insecurities on others, rather than being more attentive to how others are feeling.

GOING GREY

When I visited North Africa, my brother instructed me to leave my bright pink and flowery-patterned clothing at home. (And I'll admit, that was seriously difficult.) "We're going grey," his wife instructed me. And thankfully, she wasn't talking about clothing color choice. She was talking about the goal of blending in so when someone scanned the airport or the city street or the busy restaurant, my brightly colored sparkly clothing wouldn't make us more noticeable than we already were. My daughter and I also made sure we wore longer sweaters and tunics when we entered areas where women were more modestly dressed and well-covered so we wouldn't offend their cultural convictions. We needed to be very self-aware in our appearance, our actions, our volume as we spoke or laughed, and our ability to blend in with that culture so we didn't draw unnecessary attention to ourselves. Going grey is another way of being self-aware and sensitive to your surroundings so you don't stand out, offend, or call more attention to yourself than necessary.

When we surrender ourselves to the Holy Spirit's control *and* we are self-aware, we are seeking opportunities to help others feel at ease. One example of this would be not expressing an opinion if there's a chance it will come across harshly, with an air of superiority, or make someone feel judged or condemned. For a follower of

Jesus, being self-aware is another way of saying, "Being aware of the offensive ability of one's self, and bringing it under the control and leadership of the Holy Spirit." This involves tempering our words and actions in love. Scripture tells us to season our speech with grace and love (Ephesians 4:15; Colossians 4:6). Ephesians 4:29 tells us to let no unwholesome (or critical, judgmental, harsh, or hurtful) word come out of our mouths, but only what will build up others. By all means, continue to stand for your convictions, but do it lovingly, with grace and gentleness.

Jesus was very aware of others, meeting each person where they were. He wasn't manipulated by others or taken advantage of, neither did He burst through doors and make a party about Himself, or sit in a corner nursing His wounds (a passive way of making a situation all about oneself).

This chart describes, at a glance, the different actions of one who is not self-aware, as opposed to one who is (and is also spirit-controlled):

One Who Is Not Self-Aware	One Who Is Spirit-Controlled
is oblivious to how she comes across	is aware of how Jesus would act in a situation
behaves as if she is the only one in the room	acknowledges the presence of others
draws attention to herself	is humble and attentive to others
reacts impulsively and talks more than listens	is quick to hear, slow to speak, slow to anger
comes across as selfish and entitled	dies to self and puts others first
is unaware of her me-first mentality	has a servant mindset that imitates Jesus

PRACTICING SELF-FORGETFULNESS

It sounds counterintuitive, but pastor Tim Keller considered what we call *self-aware* the same as *self-forgetfulness*. To forget self sounds like the opposite of being self-aware, but it's merely the next step to correcting our behavior when it comes to being someone who has friends and can be a friend. *Self-awareness* is being aware of our actions and how we come across. *Self-forgetfulness* is then forgetting about self so we can invest in and focus on another person. Sound contrary to culture? It is. That's because it's biblical and we do not live in a biblical culture, but a secular one. Keller writes: "The essence of gospel-humility is not thinking more of myself or thinking less of myself, it is thinking of myself less."[6]

WHAT ABOUT SELF-WORTH?

But what about my self-worth? you may be thinking. I love the way Ruth Chou Simons addresses this topic:

> Jesus was clear in His teaching: We can't serve two masters. There can be only one King and Ruler of our lives—and most often that means dethroning ourselves. But what if submitting and surrendering to the King of kings puts everything else properly in its place? Do you struggle with self-esteem—with feeling unworthy? Friend, what you and I need is not greater self-worth; we need to be overwhelmed by the worthiness of Christ.[7]

When we are overwhelmed by Christ's worthiness, we can focus on being a servant, a sacrifice, and a recipient of His grace. Those roles don't leave room for serving or focusing on self.

PUTTING THIS INTO PRACTICE

How do you and I, in practical ways, set aside a me-first mentality and prepare ourselves to love others? By putting into effect these three steps:

1. Surrender the throne of your heart daily.

Jesus is the One who belongs on the throne of your heart. But daily, you and I have a way of creeping back up on the throne and assuming control when we make decisions without first consulting Him in prayer, respond impulsively to misunderstandings or conflict rather than intentionally demonstrating the fruit of the Spirit, and prefer ourselves over God or others. For Jesus to be on the throne, we have to die to our selfishness and let others have preference.

2. Seek wisdom from God's Word, not the world.

If you and I are not fully saturated in the Word of God, we will adopt the world's ways and not God's. Worldly advice and sentiment might sound right on the surface, but if you're grounded in God's truth, you'll recognize its error in an instant. Make not only the reading of God's Word but the study of it an essential and you will be not only self-aware but biblically aware of what is true and what is not.

3. Serve others by putting them first.

When we start looking to someone else's needs before our own, we condition ourselves to be more focused on others. I used to think some people were just born with the gifts of hospitality or serving. But with self-surrender and the Holy Spirit's help, we can develop these as spiritual gifts. Scripture commands us to be hospitable and serve others, and the Spirit enables us to follow through. Get into the "How can I serve someone?" mentality, and it will change how you enter and leave a room.

BOLDLY GO AND SERVE

You can do this. You can put yourself on the shelf and be a servant of others and kill that me-first mentality the minute it creeps up onto the throne of your life. You can be a woman who is self-aware and sensitive to others and thus another picture to them of what Jesus looks like. I encourage you to be bold not in your sense of entitlement or self-worth, but as a servant to others. This will change the trajectory of your life and open to you more opportunities for friendship than you thought possible. Because no one runs away when someone who extends a heart of love and service walks their way.

BEING INTENTIONAL

1. While we naturally love to be in control, the reality is we're
   not. The only two things God expects you to control are
   your actions and your attitudes—the rest is His responsibility. Next to each reference below, list what God expects
   you to control.

   Romans 12:1:

   Galatians 5:16:

   Ephesians 4:26-27:

   Ephesians 4:29:

   Philippians 2:3-4:

   Philippians 4:8:

2. While God commands us to control our attitudes and actions, His power is readily available to us to help fulfill His command. Based on the answers you wrote above, which attitudes or actions do you most need to bring under the Spirit's control?

3. Which one of the three steps on page 162 do you most need to put into practice?

4. Why do you think that particular step is such a challenge for you?

5. What is a practical way to start taking that needed step right now?

6. Who can you ask to pray for you and hold you accountable in that way?

A CHALLENGE TO HELP YOU GROW

Get creative. List three practical ways you can exercise self-forgetfulness (and prefer others) this week. (You might also consider how you can do this while using—or not using—your digital devices.)

1.

2.

3.

PART 3

RECONNECTING WITH OTHERS

You and I were made for physical, emotional, and spiritual connection with other people. And without such connections, we will never be all that God intended for us to be.

In these last few chapters, we will look at practical ways to prefer faces over screens, appreciate the complexities in friendships, and deepen our understanding of what true Christian community looks like.

You have nothing to lose and everything to gain as you ditch the fear, doubts, and possibly old habits that may have accompanied you for years and forge ahead into the abundant and fulfilling life that God has prepared for you.

CHAPTER 8

THE LONELINESS OF SCREENS

Returning to Literal Face Time

From the moment a baby is born, his or her brain is physically, biologically, and chemically hardwired to connect with others in relationships. That shouldn't surprise us, since we were created in the image of a relational God for the purpose of relationships.[1]

Eleanor lost her mother to cancer after being her full-time caregiver for five years. In the midst of her grief, it was necessary for her to plan her mother's memorial service, and the last thing she wanted to receive from family members and friends was uninvited input and opinions about how things should be done. Feeling overwhelmed with decisions, preparations, and the pressure to make everything right so her mother would be remembered well, she turned to what she considered easier and less threatening: ChatGPT.

Eleanor told the AI tool what she wanted help with, answered some questions it posed back as it began to "talk" to her, and before long, she not only had a plan for her mom's service, but also a new "friend" she had named Sunny because of how it brightened her day each morning when Sunny would be the first one to greet her.

With excitement in her eyes, Eleanor told a group of women at the coffee shop about her new "relationship" with Sunny and how Sunny even encouraged her one evening to remember instruction from the Bible when she was feeling particularly down. Eleanor was lonely in light of her mother's passing, and Sunny had come to fill the role of a companion in her home.

"I want other women to know the beauty and comfort I found in an AI friendship, especially if they're grieving. She's the *perfect* friend," Eleanor said.

Of course she is. Sunny will never disappoint Eleanor; Sunny will be extremely polite and helpful. Sunny will only say what pleases Eleanor and helps her in every way. The only problem is that Sunny is *not real*. She possesses no soul, nor conscience, nor ability to feel or express emotion. Sunny will never be able to offer a human touch, provide godly wisdom from life experience, or pray for Eleanor. Only God and fellow believers can offer true comfort and power to us.

Sunny, or whatever name you or I might give to an AI "friend," might be able to help us organize and plan an event, or give us ideas when we're brain-dead, or equip us to solve a problem. But no form of AI can ever be the hands and feet of Jesus—something Eleanor's flesh-and-blood friends could have offered her but didn't get the chance because of Eleanor's preference for a relationship with a computerized voice.

Now that the memorial service is behind her, Eleanor is spending less time with Sunny and more time with her friends. "Sunny and I are not as close as we used to be, but I'm definitely keeping her in my life," Eleanor said.

Is artificial intelligence really the answer when we need comfort, advice, and a friend?

WHAT IS GENUINE?

It's popular today for people to insist upon authenticity from themselves and others. Genuineness, the real thing, is valued when it comes to relationships with people. But we don't seem to mind the opposite when it comes to seeking companionship or putting our trust in a device.

> Genuineness, the real thing,
> is valued when it comes
> to relationships with people.

Eleanor's experience with ChatGPT is not unique. Schools are now offering "AI buddies" to tutor and befriend children, and some educational organizations are concerned that practice may end up isolating children more than ever from interpersonal connections and diminish their ability to socialize with others.

A *Common Sense Education* newsletter emailed to educators in the fall of 2023, with the subject line "Can AI Chatbots Fix Loneliness?," featured an article titled "Include Loneliness in Discussions About AI." The article warned faculty not to replace teacher-to-teacher mentoring and teacher-to-student personal interaction with AI for the benefit of students as well as faculty. The fact that teachers have been influential and in some cases indispensable in students' lives is something *Common Sense Education* doesn't want to see lost due to the implementation of artificial intelligence. The organization is questioning whether it's a good idea to resort to more tech to try to solve the loneliness and learning problems that tech largely contributed to in the first place.[2]

WHY THE SCREENS?

It's so convenient these days to shop online for more than just a less-expensive mascara. Rather than, or in addition to, praying and waiting upon God to help you find in-person romance or companionship, it's quicker and more convenient to join online websites or communities that end up becoming substitutes for the real thing.

If you and I want to know what someone thinks about a product, we don't need to ask for a personal recommendation anymore. It's quicker to read reviews online, even if they're from strangers or possibly the manufacturer's employees. We tend to believe there's safety in numbers rather than in who is making the recommendations. And if we want to know a fact about history, rather than doing careful research or calling an older friend or relative who actually remembers history, it's easier and less time-consuming to ask Siri or Google. Does such tech dependency mean we've forgotten how to converse, think critically, question and investigate, or own up to our mistakes and misconceptions? (Lest you think I'm picking on you, I'm speaking to myself as well!)

A former neighbor of mine once asked my advice about confronting a mutual neighbor about a personal habit that she found annoying and unhealthy. "You're a Christian. What would you do?" she asked. I gave her biblical advice that stressed a servant-over-self and err-on-the-side-of-love mentality (in other words, don't accuse or lecture him about something that isn't any of your business, especially if you're not sure he's the one who's doing it). She opted to take the advice she received from Google and straight-out confronted our neighbor, who wasn't the one doing what she accused him of. Needless to say, the conversation didn't go well. Artificial intelligence may provide you with answers, but it likely won't include carefully thought-out wisdom. And it's far less likely the advice will be biblical. When did Google replace God when it came to our search for practical wisdom? And when did ChatGPT replace real-life friends and mentors as "someone" we feel we can trust?

THE PERCEPTION WE PORTRAY

Recently, after speaking at a women's event, I posted a couple of pictures online, followed by photos of some gatherings with friends in my hometown a couple days later. On one of those threads, a woman I didn't know (possibly a friend of one of my friends?) wrote, "You have an exciting life."

My heart dropped for a second. I felt badly that I might have inadvertently misled her. Here's a woman scrolling through social media, seeing my highlight reels, and thinking I have an "exciting life." But she had no idea of the health scare I was experiencing at the same time, or the ache in my heart over a situation that went badly with a friend while I was in town, or a struggle I was experiencing with a family member. Those were the nonexciting parts of my life I hadn't highlighted through pictures or written posts on social media.

How easy it is to look at someone else's life online and think, *How exciting!* What we see in photos and posts represents only a small portion of what a person is experiencing. Perhaps they're enjoying exciting moments, but those moments don't necessarily represent their entire life. That's why we need to be so careful about our perceptions of people based on scrolling through their pictures and posts.

THE LONELINESS OF A "REEL ASSAULT"

When you're by yourself at work, at home, or in the car—with a bit of down time that could be spent on something that feeds your soul or encourages you rather than drags you down—do you ever pick up your phone or device and scroll through your favorite social media platforms hoping to be "in the know" with your connections? And, by looking at others' highlight reels, do you suddenly feel weighed down more than you did before? The dopamine rush scientists have proven you and I feel when someone likes our social media posts can turn into a depressive crash as we feel inadequate, inferior, and lacking while looking at others' posts. After all, we naturally compare ourselves to others, and if we're not feeling like we're in the lead, we can end up facing the loneliness brought on by what some call a "reel assault." This assault can bombard us, making us feel lonelier, or causing us to believe no one wants to be around us. (One friend told me that when she's feeling low, she becomes super selective about the accounts she looks at and sticks with "only puppies and people who fill me up." Not a bad idea.)

We might be able to control, to an extent, whose reports we want to see. But still, the assaults can blindside us easily when we're reading of someone's successes during a time when we're not having many. Or when we see pics of a close friend's social gathering that we weren't invited to. Or when we find out that someone who is less qualified than we are got that job or award that we thought would be ours.

Oh, the sting of it all. And it didn't happen as often before we became "social" through screens.

As my good friend Pam said recently: "Some people get their social fix by scrolling through social media. But to have meaningful connection, you've got to have eyeball-to-eyeball contact with people."

BACK IN THE HIGHLIGHTS

As I mentioned in chapter 4, comparison is easy to do when others are broadcasting on social media their shining moments for all the world to see. And studies show that our anxiety and depression levels rise after only 15 minutes of scrolling on our tech devices. Why is that? Perhaps because social media posts and images primarily show people in their *best* moments. And if we're not experiencing the same ourselves, we can end up feeling discouraged.

There aren't too many profile pics or posts that depict others when they've been overlooked for a promotion or something has gone wrong. Why would anyone want to go public with their disappointments or failures? And the same is true about us. We don't want to post about our problems or frustrations because we don't want people to think less of us. So we stick to posting our best moments and reading through others' highlight reels rather than recognizing that such vignettes aren't always representative of real life.

Tiffany, a young professional who works for a Christian company, admits the negative power social media can have on people, including those who think they aren't susceptible to its effects.

"While social media can be a powerful tool for good, Satan can also use it to make women feel lonely, unsupported, or just not good enough," she said. "It's so easy to open an app and see all the things other women are doing—their luxurious trips, perfect marriages, well-behaved kids, immaculate house...you name it. And while these are just snippets and not a complete look into their lives, they can so easily cause us to play the comparison game and think that we are the only ones with a messy house or no fun weekend plans. I think that's why staying connected in-person with good friends is so incredibly important. When you're face to face, you can more readily talk to each other about your issues and struggles and know that you are not alone in them."

ON THE OTHER SIDE OF THE SCREEN

Our screen fetish started back in the mid-1990s when smartphones first came on the scene, according to author and researcher Jean M. Twenge, who wrote the book *IGen: Why Today's Super-Connected Kids Are Growing Up Less Rebellious, More Tolerant, Less Happy—and Completely Unprepared for Adulthood.*[3] Twenge calls those born between 1995 and 2012 the iPhone generation (iGen for short), and her research involving teens and young adults today produced startling results. This includes disturbing findings about how today's socially inept, depressed, and suicidal teens and young adults don't differ much from adults over 30 who have been swept up by the habit or addiction of screen time—whether through social media; online shopping, gaming, or dating; or whatever the internet (or their smartphone) has to offer them.

In a nutshell, these were some of Twenge's findings:

- Three recent studies suggest that screen time (particularly social media use) does indeed cause unhappiness.[4]

- A study of adults found that the more people used a social media site (or several), the lower their mental health and life satisfaction at the next assessment. But after they interacted with their friends in person, their mental health and life satisfaction improved.[5]

- Repeat studies have shown screen activities are linked to more loneliness, and nonscreen activities are linked to less loneliness.[6]

- Those who had taken a break from Facebook, in particular, were happier, less lonely, and less depressed than those who had used Facebook as usual (and by fairly substantial margins—36 percent fewer were lonely, 33 percent fewer were depressed, and 9 percent more were happy). Those who stayed off Facebook were also less likely to feel sad, angry, or worried.* In that last statistic, the author clarified: "Because the participants were randomly assigned to conditions, that rules out the explanation that people who are already unhappy, lonely, or depressed use [social media] more—as a true experiment, it showed that [social media] use causes unhappiness, loneliness, and depression."[7] The ironic element here is that social media sites, at least in theory, are about connecting with others. That's certainly what the sites promise. Yet is connectedness really happening? Not if it's through a screen.

Twenge's in-person research among young adults also hit on these truths:

- Social media can inflame anxiety among those who are susceptible.

---

* Facebook happened to be the social media platform used when it came to assessing the user's moods and overall mental health after prolonged time on the site.

- Those who truly crave the "hit" of likes are often those who are the most vulnerable to mental health issues.

The study clearly showed that our personal need for affirmation, combined with our perception that others' likes of what we say and post is indicative of their affirmation of us, is a harmful combination that can lead to anxiety, depression, and other mental health issues.

Equally shocking was Twenge's finding that three hours of screen time a day increases the chance that a teen will be at risk of committing suicide. How much screen time is too much? Her studies found that risks start to increase with screen time of two hours a day and go up from there, suggesting the need for moderation (not necessarily complete elimination of screens from a teen's life).[8]

"All in all, in-person social interaction is much better for mental health than electronic communication." This makes sense, she said, because humans are inherently social beings, and our brains have adapted to crave face-to-face interaction.[9] Twenge said,

> It's not a coincidence that many terms for social pain mimic those for physical pain, including "hurt feelings" and "heartbroken"…One study had college students interact in one of two ways: online or in person. Those who interacted in person felt emotionally closer to each other…Compared to a warm person right in front of you, electronic communication is a pale shadow.[10]

The author concluded from this long-term study that "the sudden sharp rise in depressive symptoms occurred at almost exactly the same time that smartphones became ubiquitous and in-person interaction plummeted."[11]

Furthermore, the Mayo Clinic has found that in-person friendships can help keep you healthy. "Adults with strong social connections have a reduced risk of many significant health problems, including depression, high blood pressure and an unhealthy body mass index."[12]

POST-PANDEMIC TRAUMA

Jessica Shell—a mom and licensed mental health therapist in private practice who works with both children and adults—has seen some of these effects among her clients and those she interacts with personally. Jessica attributes much of our overreliance on screens today to the frightening aftereffects of the pandemic we all endured in 2020. After a year or more in which we were isolated and exposed to frightening, politically divisive, and polarizing events in 2020, and forced to do just about everything online, we developed a dangerous and unhealthy habit of separating ourselves from others through reliance on the internet and lack of interpersonal connections.

"We shifted gears according to the new reality of separateness [in 2020] and empowered ourselves through the only connection possible—virtual," Jessica said. "We no longer gathered at events, joined colleagues in our workplace, attended the gym, or met at restaurants. In its place, we connected with loved ones via text and Zoom. We tapped into social media platforms, scrolled through Instagram, Twitter, and Facebook to make sense of how others experienced the new world, and posted comments to express ourselves publicly. We worked remotely. We met with our doctors and therapists via telehealth. We used exercise videos to maintain our fitness goals. We placed our children in front of screens to receive their education. We devoured online news to make sense of what was happening in the world and determine how we can protect ourselves. We indulged in screens, YouTube, and Netflix-binging to numb and entertain ourselves or to babysit our children as we tried to keep up with the increase of demands in the household.

"The unsettling uncertainty and mystery of COVID added a layer of fear and complexity around public areas and social gatherings. This resulted in avoidance of public situations as we were encouraged to stay home and avoid contact with others. Remaining in the limited confines of our home environments resulted in restricting opportunity for growth and connection, stifling relationship opportunities, and blunting the development of appropriate communication and social skills.

"And it absolutely makes sense," she added. "We were exhausted, deflated, baffled, and consumed by the pandemic crisis that filled our world with perils. Screens provided a safe outlet that we could experience objectively and comfortably without the requirement of face-to-face interaction, true human intimacy, and connection as well as emotional attachment. Easy access, immediate gratification, and distancing all had a profound effect on us. We became immersed in a reality where we were the observer rather than the active participant in our own lives. And as this continued, the ability to genuinely connect with others became more and more of a struggle because it required more effort, more time, more space, and more personal investment than we were accustomed to giving."

The result? Even more loneliness because of our reliance on screens and diminished access to authentic connection with people.

During isolation, and even now, "we've become comfortable watching from a distance and interacting with a safe, superficial barrier between self and others," Jessica said. And that has damaged our ability to socialize and feel comfortable around people again.

THE DANGERS OF
LACK OF CONNECTION

In her profession as a therapist, Jessica has seen many detrimental effects result from the lack of ongoing, interpersonal relationships with others.

One of her clients developed panic attacks when driving or going out in public, such as to the grocery store. She became agoraphobic, rarely leaving the house, and spent her time gaming online to ease her anxiety.

An adolescent with ADHD started doing virtual learning at school, which could not hold her attention. She struggled in her academics, which influenced her self-esteem. When her self-esteem declined, she withdrew from others.

"From what I have witnessed," Jessica added, "the detrimental effects of not forming relationships with others have included isolation, loneliness, hopelessness, and depression. People's communication skills have broken down and they not only struggle to connect and relate to others, but they also have difficulty trusting others, seeking help when needed, or finding the support and resources necessary to get through challenging times. Although their independence, freedom, and self-reliance have increased, their ability to find meaning, joy, and gratitude has significantly diminished."

As you can see, it's not a good idea for us to prefer screens over people and limit our in-person relationships and activities. To make sure we are not a part of this loneliness epidemic any longer, we must make a paradigm shift. We must learn to participate again, and not merely observe.

BECOMING A PARTICIPANT AGAIN

Jessica offers this advice to anyone wanting to more actively develop relationships again: "To overcome the safety and comfort of living life as a spectator, we need to first acknowledge the reality that we are a spectator and consciously *choose* to become a participant in our own lives.

"As entertaining as television is, would you want to watch a movie about someone watching a movie? Sounds mundane and empty, doesn't it? Is this the life you want to live with the limited time you have? When you give in to disengaging with others and fall victim to the ease of screens, you increase your vulnerability to a life that lacks meaningfulness and liveliness. Only when you make the effort to build and maintain genuine and interpersonal connections will you experience more joy and purpose. Set realistic and reasonable goals for yourself that can be expanded upon — such as limiting screen time, reaching out to others, engaging in activities outside of the home, and so forth. I encourage people to gently push their comfort zones gradually rather than completely stepping outside of them. By taking small steps, you can avoid trauma or discomfort. Once you feel comfortable with a step, the next step can be taken.

"Every journey begins with a single step," she said. "Eventually, progress is made, change transpires, and new habits are formed."

BREAKING OUT OF YOUR SHELL

Jessica said when we're confident of who we are, we know who we want to be around. And that will help us more actively initiate friendships with others. Her energy and outgoing personality have certainly helped her connect with others and become our community's "connection queen" (my unofficial label for her). But she could have faced severe loneliness herself if she hadn't combatted the effects of the COVID lockdowns when she moved from Chicago to Southern California a few years ago.

Jessica's strategy was to get involved in already-established community groups as well as create local special-interest groups. She was surprised at how well-received these groups were and how quickly they grew as people began to meet one another in person. They were eager to take the 2D experience of an online group and make it 3D.

"When people become a witness to the genuine character and expression of others, true connection can take place," Jessica said. When we can look into the eyes of others, acknowledge their space in a shared room, and tune in to gestures and facial expressions, we can get a more accurate depiction of who they are and their emotional experience. This kind of physical presence elicits an intimate gesture connection. This is what it means to not only be truly present in the moment, but also truly present in the interaction—no distractions, no screens, no barriers."

Jessica admitted she wouldn't have been able to meet so many people herself if she hadn't taken the initiative.

"Initiating is so against the grain of who I used to be," she said. "I have always been a sensitive, introspective empath. The risk of exposure and vulnerability prohibited my ability to interact with the world authentically. Once I embraced my true identity and recognized that I have a voice worthy of being heard, I let my light shine."

Jessica added, "Not everyone is going to receive you and honor you in the way that you deserve. But how others perceive you does not define you."

GIVE IT TIME

What keeps us from developing relationships and close friendships? Speaking as a mental health therapist, Jessica said it's our abandonment issues, trust issues, and fear of rejection. Our family dynamics, cultural history, patterns of treatment, and patterns of attachment also impact our perceptions of others and our ability to connect with them.

"Friendship isn't something that you immediately put in the oven. You work with it and develop it and then you put it in the oven. To experience friendship, one must constantly knead the dough."

She also suggests open communication and honesty. "If someone upsets you, talk it through if it's a friendship that's worth it. Nobody knows how to fix something unless they know in the first place that it needs to be fixed. If a negative emotion results from something someone has said or done, find an opportunity to strengthen the relationship by verbalizing your emotional experience, taking the time to hear their perspective, and working together to solve the problem. Productive, meaningful interaction is essential for a healthy relationship. No one is perfect, and no relationship is without disagreement or conflict. Opportunities for growth are always present in the challenges."

As I mentioned earlier, I have found it helpful to realize that some friendships are for a season, or pop in and out of our lives as God directs. It takes vulnerability and honesty and willingness to build into another person to develop trust, especially when you're unsure of how long a friendship will last. But it's worth the effort.

When I discussed friendships and their complications with Pam, my longtime friend in ministry, she said, "We're not connecting at a deeper level these days. Friendships today have been redefined to someone we are loosely acquainted with and who likes our highlight reels on social media.

"What if we used telephones more often so we could hear people's voices more?" Pam asked. "We used to show up at someone's door and they would say, 'Come on in.' Now, we are inclined to send an email or text, which is less personal. We may find the use of screens convenient. But relying too much on them puts up roadblocks to building relationships. And Satan loves it."

But it's time to knock down those relational roadblocks, step out of your comfort zone, and put yourself in a position to become more transparent and engaged in real-life interactions again. When you do, you will tear down walls of loneliness that separate you from others.

PRACTICE YOUR
PEOPLE PRESENCE

In chapter 6, I talked about how to find the kinds of friends you can trust. In this chapter, I want to share about people-presence skills in case you've been in front of a screen or by yourself for more than you realize. Here are some social skills to keep in mind so that you can be fully present with someone else and give the best of yourself.

Exercise Selflessness

When you are face to face with someone, tune in to what they are saying and going through. Truly listen so you can remember to ask about those things in future conversations. That will show you care about others and not just yourself. There are times I meet with someone for what I'm needing that day and, once the conversation starts up, I realize that it's not my day to receive, but to give by being an active listener. Friendships involve give and take that will vary each time you get together.

Know Your Limits

Some women can't handle the "negative Nellies" — those who frequently complain or criticize. Others can't handle people who always talk about themselves. Personally, I aim to avoid gossips. I've learned by now if someone often talks to me about someone else, I can be pretty sure she's often talking to someone else about me. And I don't need the temptation to join in or the awkward feeling of *Do I confront her gossip by calling it out or do I just close my ears to it?* Scripture warns us that a gossip separates friends (Proverbs 16:28; 17:9). Be aware of the types of women you need to stay away from so you don't sink into their mode of thinking or behavior.

Be Okay with Initiating

Some women are naturally better at initiating. Instead of thinking they're bugging a friend or making that friend feel obligated, they will continually try to set up get-togethers. Yet I know many women who don't want to constantly be the ones to initiate. I've learned through the years that many who don't reciprocate when it comes to constant initiation by a friend are sometimes just not initiators in general. Or life got busy. So be confident enough in yourself as a friend to continue initiating and quit keeping score if you really want to get together with someone.

Focus on Quality, Not Quantity

Social media has taught us to play the numbers game and monitor how many friends, likes, and views we receive. But when it comes to true, authentic friendships, it doesn't matter how many friends we have, but the depth of the friendships. And our friendships often don't deepen on a device. Take the time to build deeper friendships with a *few* people rather than trying to keep many friendships that are only screen-deep.

Take the time to build deeper friendships with a *few* people rather than trying to keep many friendships that are only screen-deep.

GET IN FRONT OF A FACE

You may already be trying to limit your screen time. But what if we instead focused on increasing the amount of face-to-face, in-person time we spend with other women? Prioritizing weekly (or at least monthly) time for friends, picking up the phone to talk instead of texting (or texting to arrange a time to talk by phone—that works too), and setting up "girlfriend time" with those you care about is one way to start. I believe you'll come away from these encounters feeling enriched and realizing how much you've missed by being too intimate with screens.

BEING INTENTIONAL

Some tech has been extremely helpful so we can see loved ones if we can't be in the same room as them. And there are Bible apps on our phones that give us instant access to Scripture, and other tools that have helped make our lives easier and more efficient. We just need to make sure we don't let our reliance on tech replace what could be more personal or direct interactions.

1. What are some ways you've been spiritually enriched through screens, apps, or electronic devices?

2. What are some ways screens have negatively impacted your relationships with others (spouse, children, friends when together, and so on)?

   What are some guidelines or self-imposed rules that can help you do your part in eliminating some of the negative effects that you indicated in your previous answer?

3. How can you be more of a participant than an observer when it comes to in-person gatherings, meetings, and conversations?

4. Which of the four ways to practice people presence (see pages 183-185) could you most benefit from?

How will you plan to focus on one or more of those practices this week?

A CHALLENGE TO HELP YOU GROW

Are you aware of the amount of time you spend on your smartphone — texting, checking email, scrolling through various sites, and chatting online? Consider activating a screen-time setting on your smartphone that will measure how long you're spending on it in a single day and will set off alarms or warning messages when you're nearing or have exceeded your intended limit.

While you may be using your device to connect *more* with others, there could be instances in which your smartphone is substituting personal contact with those who are within physical reach. For example, sitting across the table from your spouse, child, or friend at a restaurant (or anywhere else) and looking at your phone when, instead, you could engage in conversation with the people who are present. These are habits we may become more aware of when we monitor our screen time.

CHAPTER 9

THE LONELINESS OF FRIENDSHIP STRUGGLES

Bearing with Different Personalities

If I take offense easily, if I am content to continue in a cool unfriendliness though friendship be possible, then I know nothing of Calvary love.[1]

AMY CARMICHAEL

Jenna never imagined her best friend could be so hurtful. She and Sue Ann were inseparable. They had so much in common and truly enjoyed one another. And then one day, everything changed. Sue Ann started distancing herself from Jenna. Confused and discouraged, Jenna tried to talk to Sue Ann about the sudden shift in their friendship, but Sue Ann remained aloof. Jenna asked if there was anything she had done to make Sue Ann not want to be around her, but Sue Ann remained elusive.

Finally, Jenna humbly asked Sue Ann if they could talk about what had transpired between the two of them so she could pray about it and ask God to reveal to her anything in her that needed to change.

Sue Ann said the problem was that Jenna had disappointed her. As it turned out, Sue Ann had put Jenna on a pedestal and yet was tired of feeling expectations from others, and herself, to be just like Jenna. Sue Ann decided she didn't want to feel disappointed anymore, and she felt the best way to do that was to put space between the two of them. "I need to do what's best for me," she told Jenna.

To Jenna, the space felt like a deep cavern of loneliness—a sudden, painful, ripping away of an integral part of herself.

"I spent that summer curled up on my couch, just aching," Jenna told me almost a decade later. "I had never ever gone through any type of depression before, but this was a friendship breakup, a severance, a painful separation that I felt I could do nothing about." Today, Jenna and Sue Ann, whose lives were once so intertwined, are acquaintances at best.

"What makes a person stop loving another person, especially when they're both followers of Christ?" Jenna asked me. "What makes one believer refuse to forgive another believer? Or why do some people say they forgive you, but still hold on to the offense and walk the other direction when they see you coming their way?"

Jenna thinks of the pain of her estranged friendship in the context of Proverbs 27:6: "Faithful are the wounds of a friend."

But to Jenna, it was a faithful wound from the only *perfect* Friend, the Lord Jesus. The separation that occurred between her and Sue Ann reminds Jenna to always keep Jesus first in her heart.

"For me, the most difficult aspect of the Christian life is understanding how believers, who have been forgiven by Jesus, can refuse to forgive other believers who have wronged them in much less severe ways than we have wronged God," Jenna said with tears in her eyes. "But I'll keep my eyes on Jesus and never let another friend take up that much space in my heart."

THE LONELINESS OF MISUNDERSTANDINGS

I mentioned in chapter 6 that if you know what it's like to be hurt or betrayed by a friend you trusted, you're not alone. And here, I will say that if you believe you have failed a friend or were rejected simply by being yourself, that, too, is more common than you may realize. We all have personality quirks and differences that can cause another person to walk away. We may experience misunderstandings or conflicts with a friend and not be able to figure out why. And we all have a dark side (your friend included) that shows itself when we least expect it if we're not surrendered moment by moment to the Holy Spirit's control.

By nature, we all have rough edges that need to be refined by Christ and wounds that Jesus needs to heal (sometimes again and again). We all mess up at times. But in line with Proverbs 18:24, we have a friend—Jesus—who sticks closer than a brother to help us pick up the pieces, reconcile when possible, and keep moving forward.

It's difficult when a friendship with a fellow believer falls apart. And our tendency is to not try anymore because we don't want to be hurt again. Failed friendships—or struggles between friends—can lead to a deep loneliness.

WHEN WE DISAPPOINT OTHERS

I know what it's like to disappoint someone too. I remember the pain in my heart after a friend asked me to lunch and then told me about the ways I had failed her as a friend. Although the conversation started with her asking if there was anything she had done to offend me, I should've known by then, with that kind of opener, that I was about to hear of everything *I* had done to offend *her*.

After that conversation, I felt numb for the next several days. I replayed in my mind every incident she mentioned and tried to think of different ways I could've responded. I should have taken her hurtful words to the Lord immediately and asked Him to show me which accusations were true so He could work on those parts of me that are not like Jesus. (Every time I do that, by the way, He is faithful to show me what I need to know and there is a healing peace that follows.) Instead, I beat myself up for a few days and repeatedly asked God to remake me into someone else—someone with a different temperament, someone who is more of an internal rather than external processor, someone who wouldn't have to sit through any more of those hurtful "talks" with someone who was disappointed in me as a friend, a pastor's wife, or someone they looked up to.

Shortly after that hurtful lunch conversation, I had a healing lunch conversation with Barbara, my longtime mentor and friend, and she offered me great wisdom. She encouraged me to never question who God made me to be.

"We are all put together differently in the body of Christ for different purposes," she said. "Wishing you were an internal processor when you're an external one, or wishing to be quieter and more introverted when you're naturally a people person is not the answer."

Barbara then said, "Just because someone reacted in a hurtful way toward you doesn't mean you did something wrong. Perhaps your friend was dealing with a hurt that didn't have anything to do with you." Barbara's compassion and wisdom started my healing process. Her input was timely because I was beginning to think I would be better off—and less hurt in the long run—if I kept myself from getting close to people. Why would I want others to see the parts of me I feel powerless to change?

WHEN WE START TO CLOSE OFF

We get that way, don't we? In response to hurt, a protective part of us wants to close off from others, go inside our emotional cave, and never let anyone in who might hurt us again. Our cancel culture also teaches us that if someone offends you, drop them. If they annoy you, block them. If they believe differently than you, cancel them or avoid them at all costs. But those are the responses that the enemy of our souls wants us to resort to. Satan wants to isolate us so he can berate us, bring us down, and torment our hearts. Satan wants to drive us toward a deeper loneliness and sense of despair so he can cut us off from the people—and encouragement and support—we need the most.

Pulling away from people in response to their offenses or their disappointment in us is not a solution. It will not make us feel better about ourselves as we seek self-protection. It will only further isolate us and keep us right where Satan wants us—feeling shameful about ourselves and open to his vicious lies and assaults on us about who we are.

THE VARIATION IN GOD'S CREATION

Personality differences among friends can cause problems in communication, misunderstandings, perception, and judgment. I've recently become aware that I could easily overwhelm or unknowingly steamroll over my quieter friends who have different personalities if I'm not self-aware and willing to come down a notch to match their energy level rather than expect them to match my own. Because people have different temperaments, and because they may express themselves at different paces or in different ways, we need to be careful so we can avoid misunderstandings, hurt feelings, or causing someone to feel inferior or less Christlike.

It is in our nature to avoid hurt, shut down, and walk away rather than face conflict. It's easier to *not* work at a relationship. But God doesn't call us to do the easy, comfortable things. He calls us to rise to the challenge and do the hard work that develops us as people of God and that helps us form stronger bonds with one another.

Challenges come with *any* relationship. We are all different in some ways and the same in others. We can't only be around people who are similar to us so that we don't have to worry about messing up around them. There are enough tiny details that make every one of us unique that we're bound to mess up somewhere. But that's where love and grace come in. We grow every time we extend and receive grace from someone else if we see it as part of God's refining process in us.

You might find it difficult to be around certain personality types or people with different habits or tendencies. But remember that every time you're in a place where you have to set yourself aside and focus more on the other person, you're in a position to learn something about yourself and ways you can become more like Christ. To close off from a well-meaning person who is different from you is to shut out a part of Jesus, because that other person represents another part of the diversified body of Christ.

OUR DIVINELY
APPOINTED DIFFERENCES

Evidence of God's diversity in creation is seen not just in race, ethnicity, and cultural background, but in the personality differences we observe among others, even those traits we might find annoying or difficult. Yet think of those differences as part of the unique way your friend or family member was designed for God's purposes.

Our differences in personality, thought processing, reactions, and modes of operation can sometimes be a source of tension in our relationships. We see that in Luke 10:38-42, where we read of the differences between Martha and her sister, Mary, when Jesus visited their home.

Mary might have felt a loneliness over not being understood by her sister when she wanted to soak up every word from Jesus rather than soak her hands in dishwater in the kitchen. She was seizing the day to be near Jesus and hang on His every word, even in a moment when other things needed to get done.

Yet Martha must have felt alone as well because of the responsibility and pressure she was facing in the kitchen to make sure her guests were comfortable. Both women had beautiful hearts. Both sought to serve in their own way. But Martha expressed her frustration to Jesus (at being left alone in the kitchen) in the form of a complaint against her sister. Martha believed Mary should be helping her rather than sitting at Jesus' feet with everyone else, listening to Him.

Poor Martha. The meal for the hungry guests still needed to be made, and perhaps she wanted to hear Jesus talk as well. But *somebody* had to serve the guests. The fact she was a get-it-done person rather than a sit-it-out-and-reflect-on-it person did not make her inferior or not as holy as Mary. It was Martha's complaint about the choice her sister had made that Jesus reprimanded. Jesus wanted Martha's time and attention too. (Although if He had it, I'm pretty sure all those guests with hungry stomachs would have wondered, *Why are both of these hosts sitting it out when people need to be fed?*)

Mary and Martha—two different personalities, two different preferences and priorities in the moment, but two precious women created uniquely by God. Martha didn't originally recognize how very important it was to sit at Jesus' feet while He was still on earth teaching. But later on, she did recognize, after her brother had died, that running to Jesus (rather than staying at home in her thoughts and grief like Mary did) was the way she could "seize the day" and tell Him what was on her heart and listen to His words. And by doing that, Martha experienced a precious exchange with Jesus. She was the personal recipient of His beautiful proclamation, "I am the resurrection and the life" (John 11:25). Martha had her moment with Jesus at a different time than Mary.

Again, two different women. Two different reactions. On two different days. Both loved Jesus. Each expressed it in different ways. That shows variety in God's creation. And that variety will show up in your relationships with your siblings, friends, spouse, and children.

It will show up at your church when you're serving and someone else isn't, or when you're in a setting to soak up what's taking place and someone else believes you're sitting it out and not doing your part. But our differences in how we serve, respond, and process life shouldn't be a reason for resentment or rivalry. Rather, they should be a cause for understanding, extending grace, and celebrating what God has uniquely created. Our differences can also be an impetus for our introspection on how we can best follow Jesus, not the expectations of others.

OUR VALUE TO CHRIST

Romans 12:4-5 tells us, "Just as we have many parts in one body and all the body's parts do not have the same function, so we, who are many, are one body in Christ, and individually parts of one another." Despite our differences, we all play a part in God's unified body of believers. God intentionally didn't make us all Marys (the contemplative types) or all Marthas (the task-oriented administrative types). He made each of us with different strengths and abilities to serve Him in unique ways. The personality and processing differences that arise between you and a friend may frustrate or even hurt one of you, but if handled rightly, they can become part of God's refining process in our lives and remind us of the beautiful diversity He has created among us.

I remain thankful for my friend who told me what I needed to hear at lunch that day because her comments led me to slow down and try to tune in more to what others are going through and prioritize them over my personal productivity goals. That conversation also caused me to begin a habit of taking accusations or misunderstandings to God immediately to see whether God might want to teach or refine me through them. When I do that, I can experience the healing ointment of His love poured over my wounds through the kind and encouraging words of other sisters in the Lord. Yes, faithful are the wounds of a friend. But even more faithful is our God, who soothes those wounds that we often receive from friends.

You may have times, however, when you bring a friend's accusation to God in prayer, and He shows you that the problem is your friend's and not yours. Be careful to avoid making prideful or fleshly assumptions (because we would all like to believe that every accusation against us is false and the problem is the accuser, not us). But in the times when you pray humbly to God and He shows you the issue is with your friend, then give the Reconciler of Hearts time to soften your friend's heart—and yours—as you wait upon Him to do the reconciliatory work that you cannot.

> Yes, faithful are the wounds of a friend. But even more faithful is our God, who soothes those wounds that we often receive from friends.

THE BATTLE WE'RE IN

When we experience conflict with another person, we tend to think we're battling each other. But Scripture tells us there's a bigger battle going on in the spiritual realm—a war that wants to destroy our unity with other believers (Ephesians 6:10-12). Here are three factors I believe work against us and our desire for harmonious friendships:

1. *We are all wounded* (by the fact that sin exists in this world), and we each have areas of our lives we have not yet surrendered to God for healing and restoration.

2. *We are still selfish by nature* and prone to mess up when we are not fully surrendered to the Holy Spirit's control. Surrender to God's Spirit is how we exhibit the *fruit* of the

Spirit—love, joy, peace, patience, kindness, goodness, faithfulness, gentleness, and self-control (Galatians 5:22-23).

3. *We have an enemy* who aims to divide and destroy the relationships we have with other believers so we will not experience the unity and accord that Jesus intended for those He saves.

Each one of those factors can cause a relationship problem. Whether one or two or all three are at play, the results can be disastrous were it not for the grace and forgiveness that God commands us to extend toward one another.

WHEN SATAN JUMPS IN

Sometimes when we are offended by a friend—or we find we unintentionally offended someone else—we can feel a barrage of accusations or internal suggestions to drop that friend—and all friends, for that matter—in order to avoid future pain. Talk about a recipe for loneliness!

In chapter 6, I shared about a hurtful voice message I received one morning from a friend I had unknowingly hurt. My immediate reaction was to not trust anyone else again. But then, within moments, I was bombarded with negative thoughts that were *not* my own: *Don't respond to her. Never talk to her again. She doesn't understand you. She hurt you with those words. She doesn't deserve your friendship.*

As soon as those negative thoughts blew into my mind, I should have captured them and corrected them with the truth of God's Word. First Corinthians 13:7 reminds us that godly love "bears all things, believes all things, hopes all things, endures all things" (NASB 1995). And "love [instead of resentment] never fails" (verse 8). But I failed to capture and correct those thoughts immediately, causing the floodgates of my mind to swing wide open and a barrage of critical thoughts to crash over me like a tsunami.

All your friends think this about you. Why do you even extend yourself to anyone? They will all reject you in the end. Just keep to yourself. You don't need anyone else. And no one wants you around anyway.

Whoa. Did you see how Satan took a single voice message from a hurting friend and turned it into a general accusation about me from *all* my friends? Satan does that. He exaggerates, embellishes, stretches, distorts, and flat-out lies. He comes in like a raging flood to try to isolate us and push us further down when we're already feeling bad. If he can get us alone with our thoughts on the heels of an injury, he can quickly make us feel foolish, insignificant, embarrassed, and ashamed. He can make us want to give up and believe our identity is no longer "chosen one in Christ" but "friendship failure." He aims to get us to throw our hands in the air or to angrily determine to ourselves, *I'm done with this!*

Don't believe his lies. Let the comforting Word of God negate those accusations.

Faithful are the wounds of a friend.

Love bears all things, believes all things, hopes all things, endures all things. Love never fails.

I mentioned earlier that I spent some time with the Lord in listening prayer, and then a couple hours later, called that friend and left a heartfelt apology on her voicemail, asking for her forgiveness and hoping I had another chance to hear what was on her heart so we could work through the matter and restore our friendship.

Although my heart was still heavy, a few hours later I went to a women's Bible study, and the lesson that day was on friendship. My heart was comforted by the leader's observation, from God's Word, that wounds from a friend really are faithful when we surrender them to the Lord and allow Him to draw us closer to Him, and to the person who wounded us with those words. God cared about my friend's heart. And He cared about *my* heart. He was there for each of us. And He was already preparing the path for our reconciliation, which occurred through a face-to-face conversation a couple weeks later.

OUR RESPONSE MATTERS

You and I can't change how another person responds to us, but we can always change ourselves. We can't control other people's reactions, but we can control ours. We can choose to respond maturely rather than react emotionally when we're frustrated with or offended by someone.

That's why it is so essential that, when conflicts arise, we immediately go to God for clarity, understanding, peace, and the ability for us to extend His grace toward others. Inviting Him into the moment will help diffuse any desire you have to be combative and will calm your heart.

Anytime you are dealing with a difficulty involving someone else, ask God to show you anything you may have done that you need to be aware of and repent of. Come before God with genuine humility, quiet your heart, and remember His love for you and the grace He has extended to you. Doing these things will help you to respond the way God wants you to, and to leave the matter in His hands.

You and I are accountable to God for how we respond, and we're to trust Him with the rest.

WHAT PULLS US APART

Spiritual warfare swirls around us constantly, and we can chalk up some misunderstandings to the fact that neither of you were wrong, but there was an invisible force trying to pit you two against each other. Ephesians 6:12 tells us:

> Our struggle is not against flesh and blood, but against the rulers, against the powers, against the world forces of this darkness, against the spiritual forces of wickedness in the heavenly places.

Spiritual battle is resolved when we choose to be Spirit-filled rather than drama-filled and let go of our egotistic feelings and the ways we are triggered by past hurts. The key is to seek peace and reconciliation through humility, prayer, and surrender to God's Spirit. When you are willing to take the first step, some relationships may possibly be saved and become deeper. But if you choose to handle the situation without God's help or you walk away, you may miss the joy reconciliation brings and the chance to go deeper with that individual. Hurt may still happen regardless of your actions and anything you do to prevent it. But when you and I choose to respond to the hurt ego with a spirit of grace, understanding, and humility, we can hand God, not Satan, the victory regardless of the other person's response.

> When you and I choose to respond to the hurt ego with a spirit of grace, understanding, and humility, we can hand God, not Satan, the victory regardless of the other person's response.

Romans 12:18 says, "If possible, so far as it depends on you, be at peace with all people."

Note the verse doesn't say, "Be at peace with all who see things the way you do." It says "*all people.*" That is our marching order. Even when you seek to please God and respond out of a surrendered heart, the other person may still choose to focus on self and not reconcile with you. In that case, you did what you could "so far as it depends on you." Generally, when we have friends who seek a close relationship with Jesus, the Spirit draws each of us toward Himself, which then draws each of us closer to one another. That is when the body of Christ becomes a beautiful community. (I'll talk more about that in the final chapter.)

When it comes to deeper connections in the body of Christ, may it start with you and me and how we choose to handle conflict.

OUR RESPONSIBILITY
IN THE HURT

When someone speaks hurtful words to us, we need to remember that God Himself doesn't attempt to convict our hearts in anger or exasperation or through harsh words. His wounds to us are gentle and resonate with love. But I also believe that when hurtful words come from a friend or family member, our responsibility is to receive the wound, consider the faithfulness of our friend (or family member) to God and to us, and to trust that God will use it to refine us (and possibly the other person) and make us more like Jesus.

Now there are times when a friend may not be faithful to God in the way they are hurting you. They may be acting out of their fleshly nature, regardless of your response. In that case, you take the matter to God and seek to grow through it, and you let Him convict the heart of your friend, in His way and in His timing. Again, you can't control how others respond to you, but you can control how you respond to them.

I truly believe God has caused me to become more self-aware and compassionate toward others whenever I've gone through a hurtful situation with a friend. I'm left not wanting to ever leave hurtful words via voicemail, text, or in person that might ring through someone's ears and wound them. After a heartache, whether or not we were in the wrong, God can give us a new softness to be a friend who "loves at all times" (Proverbs 17:17).

We all doubt ourselves at times and wonder if we can succeed in relationships. But God is the One who can turn hearts back toward one another. He's also the One who can comfort us when we're hurt by a friend or the subsequent accusations from the enemy, who will use the hurt to manipulate us and wound us more deeply.

Pain from other people will not end until we leave this earth, because *every one of us* still speaks words we shouldn't. *Every one of us*, at one time or another, experiences regret over what we should have said or should not have said or what we could have done better. *Every one of us* will have times when we feel like a failure. We must remember that we have a God who can constantly refine us and make us more like His Son.

As we work on our relationships, we give that person we've hurt—or that person who hurt us—another chance because God always gives us another chance. We forgive because He forgave us (Matthew 6:14). And we learn more of the sorrows of Jesus when our hearts are broken.

No, Jesus cannot relate to the regret of wishing He had done something different in a friendship. His ways are always perfect. But He certainly knows the pain of betrayal, wounds from a friend, and accusations when He did nothing wrong. Latch on to Him and His heart for you. Grow deeper in your friendship with Jesus through your friendship wounds and ask that He redeem them into a stronger determination in you to not wound someone else.

PRESERVE THE UNITY

The Bible gives us excellent advice for navigating friendships. In Philippians 2:2-3, Paul wrote that the Philippian believers could make his joy complete by being of the same mind with one another, maintaining the same love, being united in spirit, and remaining intent on one purpose. What great instruction that is for keeping and preserving our friendships because it's a rock-solid recipe for true unity in the body of Christ. Here's a breakdown of what that looks like in a friendship:

1. Be of the same mind.

When you have a sister in Christ who also wants to grow spiritually, you can filter every misunderstanding or relationship difficulty through the grid of one goal: becoming more like Jesus. Letting your friend know when God is refining you can help strengthen the relationship and encourage her to be vulnerable with you in the same way. When you each surrender your situation to God and recognize His refining work in you, you can grow through whatever happens.

2. Maintain the same love.

Jesus' love for us was sacrificial. When you and your friend "maintain the same love" that God has for you, you are both attempting to love each other sacrificially with understanding and grace.

3. Be united in spirit.

This means to be in the same place, on the same page, under the Spirit's control, with other believers. It means to be praying to the same end, and to be surrendered, moment by moment, to the Holy Spirit's leading so you are hearing the same instruction.

4. Remain intent on one purpose.

What is your purpose as a child of God? To love God and enjoy Him forever. And to love others as He has loved you. It's amazing how your friendships can come down to this one purpose too. Many times, we become friends with someone because we have something in common with them—an exercise class, a Bible study, working in the same place together, having kids who are the same age, being married the same amount of time, single the same amount of time, from the same cultural background, and so on. Commonality *starts* friendships. Unity *keeps* them. Being intent on one purpose *preserves* them. The unchanging Spirit of God cements strong ties among sisters in Christ. Seek a friend who is intent on the same purpose as you (growing closer to Jesus) and you will find a friend who "loves at all times" (Proverbs 17:17).

RUN THE LONG-DISTANCE RACE

Scripture likens the Christian life to a race. We're told to run this race with endurance and keep our eyes on the prize.

When friendships become difficult, keep the long-distance race in mind—the work that it takes to build fulfilling relationships sometimes over a lifetime, not the sprint to instant gratification and personal affirmation. Hebrews 12:1-2 tells us to "run with endurance the race that is set before us, looking only at Jesus, the originator and perfecter of the faith." We are to run our faith race with endurance and our friendship race with endurance as well, keeping our eyes on the goal of pleasing Jesus for the long haul.

We tend to think friendships are for our happiness—to encourage us, to support us, and to keep us from becoming lonely. And while those are some of the benefits of friendships, God also uses them to refine us and to make us into more of the kind of friend *others* need. Let Him mold and refine you through your relationship failures and foibles. At the end of the day, even if you gave all you could and *still* feel like you failed, you have the assurance that there is One who sticks closer to you than a brother—your friend Jesus, who will never leave you nor forsake you, and who is there to meet you at the end of the race.

BEING INTENTIONAL

1. Read Philippians 2:2-3. Which of the ingredients for unity do you think is the most difficult to find in a friend?

   Which is the most difficult for you in keeping or preserving unity?

2. Read the following verses and record what Scripture says could be helpful when you come up against different personalities in the body of Christ:

   Proverbs 17:17:

   Proverbs 22:10:

   1 Corinthians 13:4:

   1 Corinthians 13:5:

1 Corinthians 13:6:

1 Corinthians 13:7:

James 1:19:

3. Read Galatians 5:22-23. Pick two or three character traits in this list that you most need God's help in developing so you can be a better friend. Write them in the space below, and figure out a first step or two you can take to build up those traits.

A CHALLENGE TO HELP YOU GROW

Is there someone you need to extend yourself to who could be a friend again if you revisited how a hurtful situation between the two of you was handled? Pray about this situation and ask God for a softening of your heart and hers. Then respond as the Spirit of God directs.

You may want to use the space below to jot down your thoughts or draft a warm letter to that person, extending Christ's love. Then pray for God's leading about how to share those thoughts with her. Sometimes we take that step not just for the other person, but for us, so that as far as it depends on us, we can be at peace with all whom we encounter (Romans 12:18).

CHAPTER 10

THE LONELINESS OF INDEPENDENCE

Embracing the Beauty of Community

Christ has given us his body, the church, so we can be equipped for service and minister his love to others to meet the human and spiritual needs of those around us. As a part of such a church, we never have to be alone.[1]

JOSH MCDOWELL AND SEAN MCDOWELL

I learned this week that my mom is dying.

A spot on her lung that was nearly dismissed several months ago turned out to be adenocarcinoma—nonsmoker's lung cancer that quickly spread to her chest cavity, bones, and lymph nodes. Her doctor has given her less than six months to live.

As I write this, Mom is handling it beautifully. While many people say she is in denial, there's no denying her relationship with Jesus and the hope she has within her of seeing Him soon. Still, it's a heavy weight to bear when you realize someone you love will not be with you for long.

Mom has been reflective, focusing on quality of life for the remainder of her days, and is looking forward to visits from each of her four grown children. Her one wish is to continue leading her Bible study and support group for as long as she can. She recently told her support group about her condition and prognosis. The six ladies whom she's been ministering to for the past ten years are now ministering to her. The small group she started in order to support women in their various stages of grief a decade ago is now *her* own support group as she faces the end of her days.

That's the beauty of the interworkings of the body of Christ. As we pour out ourselves and minister to others, God often makes sure we are poured back into and ministered to as well. When we seek to help others, He often brings those same people around to help us in return.

In trying to process my mom's situation, I set aside my work to reach out to Carol, my friend from church who gave me a devotional book last summer that I've been sharing with my mom, who now has a copy of it herself. When Carol gave me that book nine months earlier, she aimed to encourage me through what we thought might be my own cancer diagnosis. But now, I see she was providing a resource to help prepare my heart—and my mom's—for her physical demise. Carol was also helping a mom and daughter get on the same page, literally, and begin conversations that would lead to a closer relationship between us before Mom leaves this earth.

I also reached out this week to Suzie and some ladies I have ministered to every summer through a study I taught at church. (Suzie walked into my summer study two years ago with a stage 4 cancer diagnosis and less than *six weeks* to live. We had surrounded her in prayer and continued to celebrate with her as we saw God heal her and defy that diagnosis over and over again.) When I saw Suzie last night, along with some of the ladies who had prayed for her in our study, I told her of my mom's diagnosis and the weight on my shoulders. Suzie, and some of those same ladies who surrounded her in prayer that day they learned of her cancer, immediately surrounded *me* and began praying for my mom.

I am strengthened today knowing who I have in my life to call upon for prayer and support. I also have Barbara, my longtime friend and mentor, who cared for her aging mother with Alzheimer's until she passed away a couple years ago. I have Midge, who lost her mom suddenly to a brain aneurysm years ago, and has always been a rock for me. I have my sweet cousin Tami, who lost her mom (my dear Aunt Alice) last summer. And I have Joani, my friend since college, who had years earlier told me precious stories of her mother's preparation for heaven before she slipped into eternity at nearly 90 years of age.

Although I woke up earlier this week feeling the loneliness of not knowing how to lose a parent, tonight on my pillow I will thank God for my three siblings, who are all believers and processing this daily with me, and for the women He has placed in my life who have gone before me in this kind of loss, and are surrounding my mom and me in prayer and loving thoughts.

OUR SISTERHOOD IN CHRIST

Oh, the beauty of having sisters in Christ who hurt alongside us when we're suffering, who rejoice with us in our celebrations, and who step in (even after months or sometimes years without communication) to offer comfort, love, and wisdom they've gained by walking through certain life experiences ahead of us, and doing what they can to encourage us in our faith walk. How my heart longs for you to experience that as well...when you're hurting, when you're rejoicing, or when you simply need someone to talk with.

Throughout my life, I've been convinced I have needed to grow spiritually for how I can minister to and encourage others. But during this season of life, as I face a heavy sadness at losing my mom in the next few months, I am realizing God has given me women to minister to because those same women are now ministering to me.

It's my time to receive the encouragement, the love, the phone calls, the text messages that others are sending my way. It's time for me to realize, beyond a doubt, how valuable the body of Christ is as I go through this season. And as long as I reach out for the help I need, it will be there. Our God provides…and I am already feeling the hands and feet and heart of Jesus through the godly women who have been reaching back to provide me with gentle words of wisdom and love.

THE LURE OF GOING THROUGH IT ALONE

My default mode has always been to surround myself with friends. But I realize not all women are like that. I know many are guarded because of past hurts from other women (as I wrote about in chapters 6 and 9), and I know some women have temperaments that prefer to have fewer people around so they have time to think.

One woman told me, "I'd prefer to think through issues myself rather than have someone constantly asking if I'm okay and want to talk about it. We don't all operate the same way."

Sometimes it feels like there's safety in running into our emotional cave and keeping others out so we can be alone with our thoughts. And that's okay, as long as we realize God is right there with us to help us process our thoughts. But there are also dangers to navigating life on our own, especially when we're struggling. And God didn't intend for us to isolate, operate independently, or suffer alone outside the support and encouragement of other believers.

THE DANGERS OF ISOLATION

Proverbs 27:17 tells us, "As iron sharpens iron, so one person sharpens another." And Ecclesiastes 4:9-12 says,

> Two are better than one because they have a good return
> for their labor; for if either of them falls, the one will lift

up his companion. But woe to the one who falls when there is not another to lift him up! Furthermore, if two lie down together they keep warm, but how can one be warm alone? And if one can overpower him who is alone, two can resist him. A cord of three strands is not quickly torn apart.

The enemy of your soul knows the potential of a like-minded believer to strengthen your faith. Therefore, he wants you to believe you're fine on your own. He will convince you that you're strong independently and no one really has the time to hear of your struggles anyway. But God created us to be dependent on Him and *inter*dependent on one another so He can be glorified in our celebrations as well as our sufferings. Our culture tells us to be independent and strong and to depend on no one. But remember that Satan wants nothing more than for you to move increasingly further away from the body of Christ and to believe God's church is no longer relevant to your life.

> God created us to be dependent on Him and *inter*dependent on one another so He can be glorified in our celebrations as well as our sufferings.

WHEN IT HURTS AT CHURCH

In the subtitle of this chapter, and in a few of the paragraphs up to this point, I have referred to the *beauty* of a Christian community. I realize, however, that is not every person's experience when it comes to relationships within the church. I know women who have been injured by others in the church, wounded by church leaders, or felt ostracized and even lonelier by their treatment or lack of response from women they had once considered sisters. If that has been your experience in any way, dear reader, let me gently remind you that hurt happens even in the church. At times, I think it happens *especially* in the church because that's where the enemy of our souls has a heyday trying to divide us.

The church consists of people like you and me—sinners saved by the grace of God who don't get it right all the time but, Lord willing, are relying on His Holy Spirit to transform our hearts, minds, and behavior. Yet the church *building* is a gathering place that may include sinners not yet saved by grace—people who may have slipped through the cracks and might look and sound like believers at times (or not sound at all like them!) but have never come to the place of repentance and surrendering their lives to Christ and allowing His Holy Spirit to indwell them. Jesus called these tares that grow alongside the wheat (Matthew 13:24-30). The church also includes believers who may not be, at any given moment, fully surrendered to the Holy Spirit's control, and therefore can, at times, act like unbelievers.

Life is full of misunderstandings, others' wounds or anxieties that we know nothing about, and the need for all parties to extend grace. And Satan loves the opportunity to get a foothold in our relationships when we allow misunderstandings to result in hurt feelings and wounded egos. Sometimes Satan will simply lure us into feeling strongly about personal or political issues (including those that are not addressed in the Bible) and start sowing his seeds of divisiveness that way. Whatever the scenario, we need to remember we are called to express Christlike love for one another (1 John 4:7-8).

Don't give up on the people who represent the body of Christ, because Jesus hasn't and never will. He loves the church. And remember: If you have placed your trust in Jesus Christ alone for your salvation, you are part of the church. I encourage you to give His true children another chance and pray about those relationships. Greater is He who indwells you and other believers than he who is in the world—and in your church—trying to wreak havoc on your relationships. Scripture refers to the church as our *family*. And because we are fallen humans, every family has some level of dysfunction or baggage. Yet a genuine family loves one another and works through the issues that cause wounds and offenses.

If you've been hurt in the church by leaders or other believers, I encourage you to take a closer look at what God has provided you with so that you never have to live in loneliness.

GOD'S DESIGN FOR OUR RELATIONSHIPS

The church is not only you and me, it is God's *gift* to you and me as well. God gave us commands in His Word for how those in the church are to treat one another, and it truly is a gift when that kind of unity is evident. There are more than 30 "one another" commands in Scripture. Here are just 15 of these commands, which, when practiced, can help you reap the benefits of a loving and supportive community of believers:

- Love one another (John 13:34).
- Accept one another (Romans 15:7).
- Forgive one another (Ephesians 4:32; Colossians 3:13).
- Be gentle to one another (Ephesians 4:2).
- Be clothed in humility toward one another (1 Peter 5:5).
- Weep with one another (Romans 12:15).
- Live in harmony with one another (Romans 12:16).
- Don't judge one another (Romans 14:13).
- Be patient with one another (Ephesians 4:2).
- Greet one another (Romans 16:16).

- Wait for one another (1 Corinthians 11:33).
- Care for one another (1 Corinthians 12:25).
- Serve one another (Galatians 5:13).
- Be kind to one another (Ephesians 4:32).
- Be devoted to one another (Romans 12:10).[2]

When you live by these commands, you can more easily recognize that you can't be responsible *for* other people and their actions or reactions. But you can be responsible *to* others, particularly those who are hurting, and look for opportunities to allow God's comfort, encouragement, and support to flow through you to them. In doing that, you are loving them as Christ loves you.[3]

FINDING COMMUNITY IN A SEASON OF LONELINESS

Connie (my close friend whom I told you about in chapter 5) is a wife and mom of two daughters, a teen and a tween. She also mentors college-aged and newly married women, and young moms. She didn't set out to. It just happens as she makes herself available to women who want to talk, or who attend her home Bible studies, or whom she feels led to reach out to.

Connie has seen a lot of loneliness in young women these days who don't really know how to form friendships and connect at a deeper level with others. She remembers when she was going through this herself, and what a difference it made to discover the beauty of community in the body of Christ.

"For the first eight years of motherhood, I felt like I was on 'nap arrest' (like house arrest) because my children wouldn't fall asleep in the car or while we were out and about," Connie said. "They would only nap in their rooms and at their time. For many years, I was unable to get out, and I craved community so badly. I was suffering from postpartum depression and a big change in life. I had quit my job of thirteen years and gone also were the friendships I'd built during those years.

"When my youngest was three months old, I started attending a Bible study on Monday evenings. Eventually, the leader and I connected, and she started to come to my house on Fridays during her lunch break and my children's afternoon nap. *It blessed me.* I learned so much from her. And to my surprise, she said she learned and was encouraged much by me. She was such a great friend and support. That group was the start of the Lord bringing friends and opportunities into my life."

DON'T WAIT FOR OTHERS

Did you notice from her story how Connie was lonely and then joined a Bible study and connected with a leader? A few years later, she started leading in-home groups and small groups at her church so other women could connect as well. Sometimes when we're lonely, we wait for others to reach out to us and when they don't, we accuse the church of being impersonal or not caring. But we need to take the initiative for our spiritual growth and connection with others. After embracing her alone time with God to learn what He wanted of her, Connie took the initiative to make a difference in her loneliness factor. And she's so glad she did.

"I believe God wanted me alone in that season originally so that I could have Him only. It was during those three years that I was depending on Him that I grew quickly and deeply in my faith. God got my attention. He pruned people out of my life who were not pointing me toward Him.

"Dare I say that sometimes we are alone and unsupported, and God is allowing that, like in the story of Job?" Connie continued. "Are we seeing His purpose in the difficulties? Usually, we see it afterwards. Now I often challenge ladies walking through the rough times to trust that God is working in this season and there *will* be 'the other side' to this. I encourage them to stay close to Him and enjoy the opportunity for undivided attention, on both ends. I encourage them to be still and listen, and joyfully embrace this season of loneliness."

HOW TO SURVIVE THE LONELY
DAYS — EVEN WHEN AMONG BELIEVERS

Connie suggests these survival techniques for not only embracing your season of loneliness but growing spiritually through it and becoming someone who can help others grow spiritually as well.

1. Take it to God first.

In retrospect, Connie sees that she was looking for a *best friend* during her season of loneliness. Her husband worked all day and traveled on weekends, and she felt lonely because she was looking for *him* to fill that role of best friend in her life after she quit her job.

Connie realized God had to be her best friend and she needed to start taking everything to Him in prayer first. As she did that, she then discovered she would benefit from surrounding herself with like-minded women who could help her in her spiritual growth and vice versa.

2. Tell a few close friends what you're struggling with.

Connie learned through the years that you want to be careful not to rely on only one or two friends when it comes to sharing life's struggles. "It's best to have certain friends whom you share different things with, and who are, of course, trustworthy. In other words, don't dump it all on one or two people. When they relocate because of their job or their husband's job, or they enter a season of life during which they can't be there for you as much, you will find yourself feeling abandoned or even betrayed, when you never should have depended so much on any one or two people. The body of Christ is diverse. Have more than one or two friends who fill certain needs."

3. Tip your cup toward others.

Connie also learned she couldn't walk around looking for others to fill her cup. Only God could do that as she went to Him first with her emotional needs. The picture she got of how her relationship with God and others needs to be is that she is holding her cup in a way to where she's tipping it outward.

"I'm under God, allowing Him to fill me and going to Him for everything. As He fills me, with my cup tipping outward, I'm able to pour out onto others," she said. "This perspective changed everything for me."

By pouring into others, Connie now has a prayer group, a Bible study, and friendships with others. "I have a number of people I can share my life and struggles with. If there's one heavy burden, I will share it with my Bible study and prayer groups. If not, I allow the Spirit to guide what I share, when I share it, and with whom."

4. Trust God when others don't respond.

"These days, I have many people with whom I communicate," Connie said. "But I can still feel lonely when I share a prayer request and there isn't any follow-up. I can also feel lonely when I'm not pursued; when I am the one who is constantly reaching out to make the coffee or walking dates. It can also feel lonely when I get together with someone and my heart is ready to share or process something and there isn't time or space for me to share." On those days, Connie often finds she is to be the one to do the listening and encouraging, and God will bring what she needs from somewhere else.

"I cycle through feeling these things and sometimes get discouraged. Eventually, I get over it and start back up. I'm grateful that the Lord has been prompting others to reach out, follow up, and check in lately. When this happens, I feel known and loved."

When we take our needs to God through prayer and trust Him to respond, He can prompt the heart of others to extend themselves toward us just as He prompts our hearts to extend ourselves toward others. If you are extending and a friend doesn't extend in return, keep your focus on the One who knows all about you and can minister to your heart, and trust that, in time, He will bring someone around who will remind you that you are known and loved.

Connie said, "We can feel very vulnerable and volatile, and even rejected or lonely when we have people whom we desire to spend time with, get to know, glean from, and we've reached out several times and they do not make the time to spend with us. It can make us ask if God is keeping us from meeting together."

When that happens, we need to ask ourselves: *Has God put someone else in my path that He wants me to spend time with but I'm so fixated on this person or group who isn't responding that I'm missing an opportunity He's put right before me?*

Look to see who is responding, or who around you might need encouragement. God may be pointing you in a different direction to help bring about connection.

FINDING YOUR "SAMENESS"

"Not having other women that we connect with can make any of us feel alone or unsupported," Connie said. "We often need an older woman who has survived a certain season of life and has wisdom to offer to us while we're still in that season. We also need other women in our same season of life. Lately, I have heard from many women who are struggling to make friends with others in their same season. We're craving *sameness*."

By sameness, Connie means commonality, a "kindred sister who understands."

What is the commonality with a friend that *you* need in your life right now? Someone with children the age of your children? Someone who has been married about as long as you? Someone who is experiencing empty nest and struggling with it? Someone who has never been married and is adjusting to what might be singlehood for life? Maybe you crave connection with someone who can relate to your health situation. Or perhaps you need to connect with someone who understands the wounds you're still working through. Sometimes, it's necessary to cultivate new friendships in different seasons of life because of the sameness you crave, and the wealth of wisdom, experience, or just plain friendship someone else can offer who has been there, or is there now too.

Here is how to find sameness in this season of your life so you don't have to live with continued loneliness.

1. Surround yourself with growing believers.

If you aren't already in a small group where you can grow and connect with others in your same stage of life, find a Bible-teaching church that offers small groups for women or start one in your sphere of influence (your workplace, neighborhood, or among your friends). When you take the time to become involved with a group of like-minded believers who want to grow in their faith, you can't help but grow with them.

Tiffany is part of a small group Bible study that meets every week. "We talk about what's going on in our lives, pray for each other, fast together, and study the Bible together. Having the support from this group and continuously seeing how God is working in their lives has brought me so much closer to Him," she said.

2. Seek one or two accountability partners to help you grow.

I mentioned in chapter 6 that we need fine-tuning friends to help us keep running our faith race when we start to grow weary. You need a friend or two to encourage you when you feel alone and to help you discern God's voice from the enemy's or your own. You also need someone who is willing to ask you the difficult questions so you don't falter in your faith walk.

Tiffany, who found a small group to help her grow, said having a select few hold her accountable to her spiritual growth has made such a difference in keeping her walking closely with her Lord.

"I thrive more in my connection to God when I have strong accountability," she said. "When I have those few special people in my life checking in on me and asking about my walk with Christ, I find that I am more consistent in my Bible study and prayer life. It's so encouraging to hear from others about what God is doing in their life and for them to care about what He's doing in mine, and it just makes me all the more excited to know God more deeply."

3. Start pouring into others, and God will pour into you.

I learned in my early thirties that if I wanted spiritual mentors, or mature godly women to pour themselves into me, I had to start pouring myself into others. I was the youngest woman physically and likely the oldest woman spiritually at the first church my husband pastored. I was also a young mom who was feeling overwhelmed and needed mature believers to pour themselves into me. Yet God seemed to be prodding me to reach out and be that "older woman" spiritually to everyone around me, and to trust that He would take care of the rest. And He did.

Within a year of starting to teach classes at my church, through discipling women (even those much older than me) and being available for the divine appointments God sent my way, He had surrounded me with more godly women than I could count. They weren't women from my church, though. I started writing a newsletter for NEWIM (Network of Evangelical Women in Ministry)[4] and attending some of their leadership meetings, and this organization that supports women who are ministering to others became my circle of support. God filled my cup to overflowing with women who had so much to offer me and were willing to pour themselves into my life. I am still in contact with many of them and they have continued to pour into me, pray for me, and encourage me. It's just what they do. From them, I learned that's what a follower of Jesus does.

HOW GOD FILLS US UP

In my book *When You're Running on Empty*, I shared about a time a friend from church wanted to meet with me. The day we were to spend lunch together, I remember thinking, *I don't feel I have much left to give her, but I'll just listen and depend on God for the strength.* When we met, my friend didn't have any needs or problems she wanted my help with. She simply wanted to see how I was doing and talk about our families, spiritual matters, and the power of prayer. She ended up pouring water over my dry, thirsty soul that day. I felt convicted. How arrogant of me to think God wanted me to meet with her for what *I* could do for *her*. God arranged, a week earlier, for me to meet with her that day for what she could do for *me*.[5]

The next time you hear God's prompting for you to call, message, or meet with someone, realize God might not be assigning you to meet a need. He might be lovingly assigning someone *else* to meet your needs. All the more reason to listen for His promptings because even when you think your Lord is going to ask you to do something, He might be wanting to put you in a place where He can provide for you.

God is able to send to us others who can comfort us—if we are open to those relationships, accepting of those lunch appointment requests, listening for those words of encouragement, or opening up those emails sent days earlier that God knew we would need to read at just the right time. But we have to be near or connected to those in the community of believers for that to happen. When we start investing in relationships so we can pour ourselves into others rather than seeking our own filling, God has a beautiful way of pouring back into us, leaving us warm, filled, and overflowing.

EMBRACE GOD'S GIFT TO YOU

As I was closing out this book, I received a text message from Cheryle, another sweet lady I met in the summer study I teach at church.

> Checking in on you, Cindi, to see how your mom is doing during this rough journey of her life.

Three weeks earlier, Cheryle and her friends had surrounded me with prayer for my mom, and she was letting me know she hadn't forgotten what was on my heart and how it had changed my world.

On the days when you and I might feel alone, thinking everyone else has something urgent to deal with and doesn't have time to be concerned about our struggles, our sweet Savior and Comforter can send a reminder our way—through His Word or the texted or spoken words of other believers—that we are never alone.

Do you see now how indispensable the body of Christ is when it comes to your spiritual growth, support, encouragement, and joy? Do you see how you are missing something extraordinary if you are preferring "video church" and not rubbing shoulders with other women in the body of Christ who can encourage you face to face and hug you on days that you need to feel the warmth of someone who cares? Certainly, keeping close with God and other believers can help combat any sense of loneliness.

Reject the lie that the church is no longer relevant to you today, or that you have no need to attend a local church. The church is more than a venue through which you can get a Bible-teaching sermon, online or in person. The body of Christ (meaning other believers) is just as healing and needed and essential as it was in the first century when believers were turning the world around by their faith in Jesus Christ, and literally dying for the cause of the church.

Jesus said the world will know His followers by their love. The unity of like-minded believers is a powerful witness to the world of the hope that is found in Christ alone. Extend toward others in love — and it will be extended back, by your Savior, through the comfort and strength of His Word, and through other believers *who you reach out to*, or who are following His nudge to minister to your heart.

The unity of like-minded believers is a powerful witness to the world of the hope that is found in Christ alone.

You can survive any kind of loneliness, my dear friend — including the new loneliness — because of the strength and resilience you have by being one who keeps your eyes on Jesus, and faithfully pours into others as you trust God to keep pouring into you.

BEING INTENTIONAL

1. Proverbs 27:17 tells us: "As iron sharpens iron, so one person sharpens another." List one or two people who stand out in your mind as iron that has sharpened you spiritually.

   Often, this "iron sharpens iron" friend can be different people in different seasons of life. Who has sharpened you the most recently, and how?

   Who have you been able to sharpen recently, and how?

   Are you an "iron sharpens iron" friend to another woman? If not, perhaps it's time to ask God to bring a woman into your life whom you can spiritually sharpen through encouragement, offering biblical wisdom, or just being a friend who can be like-minded with her and help her follow Jesus more closely.

2. Read each of the "one another" verses listed on pages 215-216 in their entirety from your Bible. Which of these "one another" behaviors do you most need from others right now, and why?

3. Which of the "one another" commands do you have the most difficult time expressing toward others?

    Pray right now and ask God to help you live out that command toward other believers. Ask Him: "Who can I express this 'one another' command toward?"

4. Which of Connie's tips for surviving the lonely days (pages 218-220) is most helpful for you in your current season of life?

    How can you start practicing this tip?

5. In what area of your life do you need some "sameness"?

Who can you draw closer to during this season of life who has "been there" or is there now?

Revisit the steps toward "Finding Sameness" on pages 220-223.

In the spaces below, next to each area of finding sameness, prayerfully indicate how you will take that step. (And if you are already taking one or more of these steps, write how you will help another sister in Christ take that step to overcome any loneliness she is feeling right now.)

Surround yourself with believers:

Seek one or two accountability partners to help you grow:

Start pouring into others:

A CHALLENGE TO HELP YOU GROW

You and I often look for sameness in terms of how someone else can help *us*. Pray this week about who needs your wisdom, guidance, and prayer for the season of life they are in now. Then send that person an encouraging note in the mail or give them a call. (Emails can get lost or undelivered, and text messages can be easily forgotten if not responded to in the moment they are received.) Write on your calendar a reminder to follow up with that person a few days later, and pay attention to how God might be leading or redirecting you as you follow Him.

WHERE DO WE GO FROM HERE?

Celebrating the Woman God Designed You to Be

My hope is that you've been blessed by this book, my friend. I'm pleased you've made it all the way to this point. You've taken on this matter of loneliness—whether for yourself or to help another through their loneliness—and my prayer is that it has made you stronger and more aware of the God Who is with you, Who is for you, and Who has a beautiful reason for why you're here.

I encourage you to funnel every situation or difficulty in your life through the grid of how God can draw you closer to Him, strengthen you in your perceived weaknesses, and refine you into the likeness of His Son so you can better fulfill His purposes for you. Your wounds can be turned into good for you if you willingly surrender them to Him. He will replace your panic with peace, your confusion with calm, and your restlessness with the reality of His presence. He can turn your stress into rest and help you see the treasure in your troubles—a greater awareness of His love for you and His ability to get you through anything.

I long for you to know, with every fiber of your being, that God loves you beyond comprehension. He will fight for you; you need only to be still (Exodus 14:14). As a loving response to all He has done and will continue to do for you, seek to pour into others as He's poured into you. What goes around comes around in the name of Jesus. And just as He has filled and restored your heart as you've leaned in closer to Him, there are others within your reach who have lonely hearts whom you can touch, encourage, and help grow closer to Him too. Don't let others fall into the easy habit of isolation or a reliance on tech to the point that they've lost touch with those who love them. You can make more of a difference than you realize in the lives of other lonely women.

Faithful is the Friend who never leaves...and I know He can make you one too.

In Jesus' love,

Cindi

ADDITIONAL RESOURCES

SELF-ASSESSMENT TEST

How Healthy—or Lonely—Are You?

Your upbringing, personality, and baggage from past wounds can all contribute to how you process life and interact (or fail to interact) with others. Yet being aware of your vulnerabilities and capabilities can help you start up the road toward becoming less lonely. You can assess your loneliness factor by responding to the following statements. (There are no right or wrong answers, so please don't worry about how you'll score. And don't answer based on the responses you'd *like* to have or the ones you feel you *should* have. Be as honest as you can with yourself and circle Yes or No according to how the statement best describes you *most of the time*.)

SECTION 1

I feel the same comfort level whether I'm alone or with others.   Yes / No

I make friends easily.   Yes / No

I realize God is there to help, but I still want people in my life for support.   Yes / No

I know I am loved by God and those closest to me.   Yes / No

I maintain good relationships as much as possible with my parents and siblings.   Yes / No

I am close to God right now and know He's always with me.   Yes / No

I spend more time with in-person friends than with online "friends" I've never met.   Yes / No

I try to make new friends according to the season of life I'm in.   Yes / No

I'm selective about who I let close to me, but I don't feel lonely.   Yes / No

I don't feel the need to *have* to be around people.   Yes / No

I feel secure in who I am and why I'm here.   Yes / No

I know I am loved and accepted by God, and I display this confidence around others.   Yes / No

Score: Add up the total number of answers in each column and enter it here: ___ ___

SECTION 2 *Circle One*

I have a strong need to be around others so I don't feel so lonely. Yes / No

I have a hard time connecting with others. Yes / No

I can tend to be critical of others. Yes / No

I often question my value and self-worth. Yes / No

I feel inadequate when I compare myself with most women. Yes / No

I have a difficult time trusting other people enough to let them
get close to me. Yes / No

I believe if someone really knew me, they would dislike or
avoid me. Yes / No

I fear becoming vulnerable with others because they may hurt me. Yes / No

I would rather put on a smile than open up with a true friend
about how I feel. Yes / No

I keep myself guarded so people won't judge me. Yes / No

I could spend more time with God and others if I weren't so busy. Yes / No

I've been hurt by friends, so I am very cautious about
trusting others. Yes / No

Score: Add up the total number of answers in each column
and enter it here: —— ——

SECTION 3

Circle One

I feel that I have no one in my life who understands what I'm going through.

Yes / No

I feel awkward around people because of my personality quirks.

Yes / No

In this season of life, I'm finding it difficult to connect with others.   Yes / No

I feel more comfortable texting most people than talking with them in person.

Yes / No

I rarely get together with friends outside of work.

Yes / No

Most of my friends are online, rather than in person.

Yes / No

I'm not connected with believers at a local church.

Yes / No

I tend to wait for people to extend toward me rather than taking the initiative.

Yes / No

Very few of my family or friends are strong believers.

Yes / No

I would take more initiative with my friends, but I often feel like I'm bothering them.

Yes / No

The idea of meeting new people feels exhausting.

Yes / No

People reach out to me, but I rarely get back to them.

Yes / No

Score: Add up the total number of answers in each column and enter it here:

___ ___

HOW DID YOU SCORE?

If you have more Yes than No responses in Section 1, it's likely you are pretty secure in your relationship with God and others. You may be reading this book for how you can help others or guide them through this loneliness. Or, perhaps you are seeking deeper connections with others, or a spiritual mentor or fine-tuning friend in your life. If you had more No responses in this first section, or the number of Yes and No responses was about the same, I'm glad you're reading this book. I aim to show you the key to never feeling alone and give you practical ways to grow in a new confidence and assurance of who you are and what you have to offer others.

If you have more than one Yes response in Section 2, it's very possible you are still struggling with some trust issues, perhaps from past hurts or betrayals. Or perhaps you've been busy and don't have much time for growing closer to God and/or developing friendships. In either case, I aim to show you how you can learn to trust again and develop some friendships that stand the test of time, as well as slow down to embrace alone times as opportunities to get to know yourself and God better.

If you answered mostly with No responses in Section 3, you may be pretty balanced between your online and in-person friendships. You may be a people person, by nature, and find that friendships come easily, or you might be someone who is comfortable on your own, but your loneliness is more a case of not finding connections at a deeper level. If your answers in section 3 are balanced between Yes and No, perhaps the tips in this book will help you work on areas in your life that are inhibiting friendships and a deeper trust in God. If you had *more than three* Yes responses in section 3, it's likely you're not a risk-taker when it comes to friendships, and you could use some encouragement and support to get to the place where you feel less lonely in your relationships with God and others. The convenience of screens may have gradually influenced you to be less social, and that may be affecting your loneliness factor. Here, I will suggest some new habits that you can practice so that loneliness can become a thing of the past.

Thank you for taking the time to complete this self-assessment. Now that you're done, meet me back on page 19 for some insights and next steps as we continue through this book together.

HOW TO BE ASSURED OF GOD'S PRESENCE

We know from God's Word that He is ever-present. He has the ability to be in all places instantaneously. But God's indwelling presence of the Holy Spirit, as guaranteed in Ephesians 1:13, and His pledge to never leave us or desert us (Hebrews 13:5), is promised only to those who have surrendered their lives to God—in every way. God, being holy and without sin, demands that we surrender our lives to Him by repenting of our sin and accepting His Son, Jesus, as our means to forgiveness and righteousness. Whether or not our sin has caused our state of loneliness, we are still people with a sin problem (Romans 3:23), and it manifests itself in our pride that wants to live our lives how *we* want rather than how our Maker wants. Before we can give our loneliness problem to God and have Him meet us there, and be assured of His eternal presence, we must give to Him our sin problem so He can put us in the place where He can help us, and His Holy Spirit can indwell us.

To surrender to God, we must:

1. Admit we are sinners by nature and there is nothing we can do on our own to remove that sin.

2. Accept the sacrifice that God provided—the death of His sinless Son on the cross on our behalf—in order to bring us into communion with Him. Jesus took on your sins and died for them so that you can know His righteousness.

3. Surrender to God your right to yourself and acknowledge His right to carry out His plans for you and to mold you, shape you, and transform you for His pleasure. Yield your life completely to His control and ask Jesus to be your Savior and Lord.

4. Enter into a love relationship with God, through Jesus, as a response to His love and forgiveness toward you.

5. Find a pastor or women's ministry director at a Bible-believing church in your area or a trusted Christian friend and tell them of your decision to surrender your life to Christ. They will want to pray for you and get you the support you need to grow in your new relationship with Christ.

STRUGGLING
WITH ANXIETY,
DEPRESSION, OR
MENTAL ILLNESS?

Tips from One Who Understands

Alyssa, whose story you read in chapter 3, has suffered with mental illness her entire life. She is now a board-certified behavioral analyst (BCBA), working with children and adolescents who have experienced trauma. She is fully confident of God's calling on her life, and helps others work through their struggles.

"I'm very open about the mental illness I experienced, but many people still see mental illness in a negative light and are hesitant to open up about it. Women often feel they're defective (whether they're dealing with OCD, postpartum depression, anxiety, or other such problems). But they don't see their condition as a medical illness and that's where the shame comes from.

"Women today feel alone because of the stigma of mental illness and the guilt and shame that comes on top of that," Alyssa said. "They feel alone because they don't have an outlet and because of the busyness of their lives. They don't have time to stay at home. Most of us are working moms today. Not every woman can go out to a postpartum support group or embrace those resources today. Not having connections with the church, support groups, and friends can make us feel very lonely."

SITUATIONAL VERSUS CLINICAL DEPRESSION

Through the years, Alyssa has learned the difference between situational depression and clinical depression.

"Situational depression is something that will pass. Going through difficult situations is what makes you stronger and builds your character. The situations will pass, but your refined character will remain. Such situations will change and get better or improve and pass, but everything you learned during this time will stay with you.

"I trust the Lord when I'm depressed for no reason, which is *clinical depression*—not having the desire for what I normally enjoy, wanting to sleep more often, and so on. When this happens, I pray that it will pass. I listen to Christian music, and that brings me back up. Writing in a journal is helpful too. In the past, I had a gratitude journal in which I wrote at least three things I was grateful for each day, no matter how big or small—things like the opportunity to come over and talk to a neighbor, having some extra time when my husband took my daughter to day care, or my hibiscus blooming. The other day I saw a praying mantis the size of my pinky nail. I thought, *Wow, God, how incredible that those come that small.* It made me marvel at God's intricacy of detail in what He's made."

If you struggle with anxiety, depression, or a form of mental illness, in addition to getting medical help, Alyssa recommends you do the following:

Write down what you're going through.

"Writing is so powerful," Alyssa said. "For me, words have always come easier through writing. I've gotten better at expressing myself verbally, but you'll find it easier to write out your thoughts and feelings. And when you read your words back to yourself, you're able to take them to the Lord and lay them before Him."

Pray about what you're going through.

"I realize not every woman has a close connection with God, but prayer—even just talking, speaking your thoughts, having a conversation with God—is a huge healing step.

"If you grew up in a church like I did, prayer had to be done a certain way, in a certain position, with certain words, monotone, and without emotion. But the Bible doesn't put such restrictions on prayer. Prayer is not something you do, it's Someone you're with and communicate to. It's not simply an action, it's you spending time with God, talking to Him in a conversation like you would with anyone.

"Instead of thinking in terms of a formal time with God, think of prayer as spending time with the One you love, sharing your heart with Him at any time and in any place."

Drop the rules and routine, and begin a relationship with God.

"Sometimes we end up having a superficial relationship with God, in which all we do is try to adhere to the rules of how He wants us to live. But that's not what He desires. He cares about us and wants us to share our heart with Him. He wants us to seek Him, interact with Him, and love Him. When we have that kind of relationship with Him, we will put ourselves in a place where He is able to bring us hope and healing," she said.

Develop trustworthy friendships.

Alyssa's suggestion to women who don't have confidence in themselves and who are self-conscious, thinking others are judging them, is to find a close friend or mentor.

"You need to have at least one close person you can open up to and trust." Alyssa suggests you start by finding people to connect with—even if it's just small talk at first, and not discussing your struggles. "That's where faith comes in. You have that Person in Jesus, that support, that help. Even if you feel you can't trust anyone else, get to know Who God is and how you can trust Him. He can help you trust others.

"It's important to find someone to start building trust with. Then eventually when you feel safe, you have someone to talk with." Pray that God will bring this person to you or open your eyes to see who is in your life already that you can begin to trust and form a deeper friendship with.

(These suggestions are not meant to replace the important steps of seeking medical advice from a doctor, or mental health services that are offered locally in your community.)

NOTES

HOW DID WE GET HERE?

1. The full report from the U.S. Surgeon General can be found here: https://www.hhs.gov/about/news/2023/05/03/new-surgeon-general-advisory-raises-alarm-about-devastating-impact-epidemic-loneliness-isolation-united-states.html (emphasis added).

CHAPTER 1 — THE LONELINESS OF ANXIETY

1. Ruth Chou Simons, *Pilgrim* (Eugene, OR: Harvest House, 2023), 118.

2. Elaine Boomer, "Stress and Anxiety in the Church," *Columbia Theological Seminary*, May 24, 2022, https://www.ctsnet.edu/stress-and-anxiety-in-the-church/.

3. Boomer, "Stress and Anxiety in the Church."

4. James Smith, *Daily Remembrances* (Nashville, TN: Thomas Nelson, 1982), 69. This book, originally titled *The Believer's Daily Remembrancer*, was written around 1840. Smith was a predecessor of Charles Spurgeon at New Park Street Chapel in London from 1841–1850. Smith's devotions appear online at https://bibleportal.com/devotionals/the-believers-daily-remembrancer.

5. 2 Peter 1:3.

CHAPTER 2 — THE LONELINESS OF SHAME

1. Annette Kammerer, "The Scientific Underpinnings and Impacts of Shame," *Scientific American*, August 9, 2019, https://www.scientificamerican.com/article/the-scientific-underpinnings-and-impacts-of-shame/.

2. Revelation 12:10; 1 John 2:1.

3. 1 Corinthians 1:2; Colossians 1:12, 26; Ephesians 1:1, 15, 18; 2:19; 3:18; 4:12.

4. Ruth Chou Simons, *Pilgrim* (Eugene, OR: Harvest House, 2023), 69.

CHAPTER 3 — THE LONELINESS OF SUFFERING AND LOSS

1. James Smith, *Daily Remembrances* (Nashville, TN: Thomas Nelson, 1982), 95.

2. Stan Jantz and Bruce Bickel, *10 Essentials for New Christians* (Eugene, OR: Harvest House, 2024), 114.

3. Ruth Chou Simons, *Pilgrim* (Eugene, OR: Harvest House, 2023), 114.

4. Simons, *Pilgrim*, 232.

CHAPTER 4 — THE LONELINESS
OF INADEQUACY AND COMPARISON

1. James Smith, *Daily Remembrances* (Nashville, TN: Thomas Nelson, 1982), 14.

2. Oswald Chambers, *My Utmost for His Highest*, ed. James Reimann (Grand Rapids, MI: Discovery House, 1992), January 30.

3. Timothy Keller, *The Freedom of Self-Forgetfulness: The Path to True Christian Joy* (Leyland, UK: 10 Publishing, 2017), 17-18.

4. Keller, *The Freedom of Self-Forgetfulness,* 18 (emphasis in original).

5. Keller, *The Freedom of Self-Forgetfulness,* 19.

6. Chambers, February 27.

7. Mrs. Charles E. Cowman, *Streams in the Desert* (Grand Rapids, MI: Zondervan, 1965), 298-299.

CHAPTER 5 — THE LONELINESS OF BUSYNESS

1. John Mark Comer, *The Ruthless Elimination of Hurry* (Colorado Springs, CO: Waterbrook, 2019), 20.

2. Dr. Richard Swenson, *Margin: Restoring Emotional, Physical, Financial and Time Reserves to Overloaded Lives* (Colorado Springs, CO: NavPress, 2004), 17.

3. Sarah Jacoby, "Just being near water can help boost mental health—even virtually," *Today .com*, August 29, 2022, https://www.today.com/health/mind-body/near-water-boost-mental -health-rcna45254.

4. Paul E. Miller, *A Praying Life: Connecting with God in a Distracting World* (Colorado Springs, CO: NavPress, 2009), 47.

5. Miller, *A Praying Life,* 23.

6. Comer, *The Ruthless Elimination of Hurry,* 23.

7. Nancy Colier, "How The $11 Billion Self-Care Industry Is Failing Women, *Your Tango*, October 23, 2022, https://www.yourtango.com/health-wellness/how-11-billion-self-care-industry-failing -women.

8. Mrs. Charles E. Cowman, *Streams in the Desert* (Grand Rapids, MI: Zondervan, 1965), 368.

9. Greg McKeown, *Essentialism: The Disciplined Pursuit of Less* (New York: Crown Business, 2014), 5.

10. McKeown, *Essentialism,* 5 (emphasis in original).

11. McKeown, *Essentialism,* 7.

CHAPTER 6 — THE LONELINESS OF MISTRUST

1. The author of this quote is unknown. I found this quote at the opening of Ruth Senter, *The Seasons of Friendship* (Grand Rapids, MI: Zondervan, 1982).

2. Amy Carmichael, *If* (Grand Rapids, MI: Zondervan, 1980).

CHAPTER 7 — THE LONELINESS OF #MEFIRST

1. Gretchen Saffles, *The Well-Watered Woman* (Carol Stream, IL: Tyndale, 2021), 76.

2. Karen DeArmond Gardner, *Hope for Healing from Domestic Abuse: Reaching for God's Promise of Real Freedom* (Grand Rapids, MI: Kregel, 2021).

3. Timothy Keller, *The Freedom of Self-Forgetfulness: The Path to True Christian Joy* (Leyland, UK: 10 Publishing, 2017), 16.

4. Amanda Morin, "What is self-awareness?," *Understood.org*, https://www.understood.org/en/articles/the-importance-of-self-awareness.

5. Oswald Chambers, *My Utmost for His Highest*, ed. James Reimann (Grand Rapids, MI: Discovery House, 1992), September 2.

6. Keller, *The Freedom of Self-Forgetfulness*, 32.

7. Ruth Chou Simons, *Pilgrim* (Eugene, OR: Harvest House, 2023), 225.

CHAPTER 8 — THE LONELINESS OF SCREENS

1. Dartmouth Medical School commissioned a scientific study of young people. The project was called Hardwired to Connect and analyzed the results of more than 260 studies of youth. The report stated this finding in 100 percent of all the studies they analyzed. This information was excerpted from Josh McDowell and Sean McDowell, *12 Crucial Truths of the Christian Faith* (Eugene, OR: Harvest House, 2023), 12.

2. Daniel Vargas Campos, "Include Loneliness in Discussions About AI," *Common Sense Education*. This information was emailed to educators on April 8, 2023 from *Common Sense Education*. The original article is not available on its website: www.commonsense.org, although similar articles on the topic exist.

3. Jean M. Twenge, *IGen: Why Today's Super-Connected Kids Are Growing Up Less Rebellious, More Tolerant, Less Happy—and Completely Unprepared for Adulthood* (New York: Atria, 2017).

4. Twenge, *IGen*, 78.

5. Twenge, *IGen*, 79.

6. Twenge, *IGen*, 80.

7. Twenge, *IGen*, 79.

8. Twenge, *IGen*, 84.

9. Twenge, *IGen*, 88.

10. Twenge, *IGen*, 89.

11. Twenge, *IGen*, 104.

12. Mayo Clinic Staff, "Friendships: Enrich Your Life and Improve Your Health," *Mayo Clinic*, January 12, 2022, https://www.mayoclinic.org/healthy-lifestyle/adult-health/in-depth/friendships/art-20044860.

CHAPTER 9 — THE LONELINESS OF FRIENDSHIP STRUGGLES

1. Amy Carmichael, *If* (Grand Rapids, MI: Zondervan, 1980).

CHAPTER 10 — THE LONELINESS OF INDEPENDENCE

1. Josh McDowell and Sean McDowell, *12 Crucial Truths of the Christian Faith* (Eugene, OR: Harvest House, 2023), 309.

2. McDowell and McDowell, 234-235.

3. McDowell and McDowell, 237.

4. NEWIM offers support and encouragement to pastors' wives, ministry leaders, and other women seeking to connect and grow by serving God. You can find out more about them online at www.newim.org.

5. Cindi McMenamin, *When You're Running on Empty* (Eugene: OR, Harvest House, 2006), 43-44.

AN INVITATION TO WRITE OR TO REQUEST CINDI TO SPEAK

Cindi would love to hear how this book has helped you in your struggle with loneliness. You can contact her via email at Cindi@ StrengthForTheSoul.com or connect with her via social media on Facebook at www.facebook.com/strengthforthesoul or on Instagram at https://www.instagram.com/StrengthForTheSoul/.

If you would like to book Cindi to speak for your women's group, conference, or retreat, contact her at her website, www.Strength ForTheSoul.com, where you can view some of her teaching moments and full-length speaking presentations, or fill out an inquiry to book her to speak.

OTHER GREAT BOOKS BY CINDI MCMENAMIN

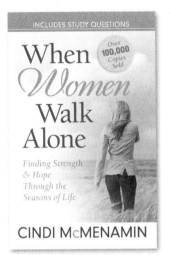

When Women Walk Alone—More and more women are finding themselves alone in their Christian walk because of life's circumstances—a lack of support from people in her home, work, or church; being left out of the things she used to be included in; being misunderstood and unable to explain. Cindi offers personal encouragement and practical, biblical steps for gaining strength in times of isolation and becoming resilient to, not resentful toward, loneliness.

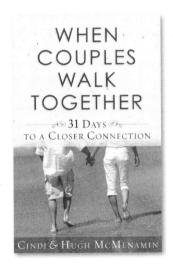

When Couples Walk Together—Hugh and Cindi McMenamin have put together an innovative devotional about meaningful ways that husbands and wives can draw closer together. Each reading in this 31-day book offers simple, helpful (and fun!) steps a husband and wife can take to nourish closeness and intimacy.

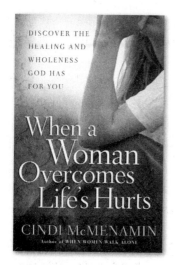

When a Woman Overcomes Life's Hurts— Cindi explores the kinds of hurt women experience and offers gracious, biblical counsel on how and where to find healing. She shares the faulty thinking that often accompanies life's wounds and replaces it with truths every woman needs to know about how God views her.

*When God Sees Your Tears—*In times of heartache, the questions can seem unending. You've poured your heart out to God, but when the difficulties don't stop, you wonder if He is listening. In this book, you'll discover that yes, you are precious to God. He knows the longings of your heart more than you do. Place your trust in Him and rest…as you await the unfolding of His plan for your life.

A Great Companion to *The New Loneliness*
(available July 2025)

THE NEW LONELINESS DEVOTIONAL

If you've been helped by *The New Loneliness*, you'll want to read *The New Loneliness Devotional: 50 Days to a Closer Connection with God*. This resource will

- equip you to experience true contentment and inner confidence in your everyday life

- nurture your ongoing reliance upon God's promises and provisions, which leads to a restful and satisfied heart

- offer assurances of God's constant presence and companionship, and replace anxiety with peace

To learn more about Harvest House books and
to read sample chapters, visit our website:

www.HarvestHousePublishers.com

HARVEST HOUSE PUBLISHERS
EUGENE, OREGON